P9-DCW-272

School Violence

Other Books in the Current Controversies Series

Capital Punishment

Censorship

Developing Nations

Drug Trafficking

Espionage and Intelligence

Food

Globalization

Health Care

Homosexuality

Illegal Immigration

Information Age

Mental Health

Online Social Networking

Pollution

Sex Offenders and Public Policy

Suicide

The Abortion Controversy

Violence Against Women

Violence in the Media

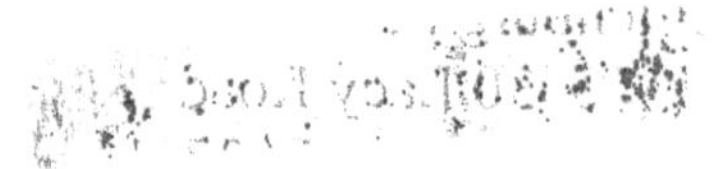

School Violence

Lucinda Almond, Book Editor

GREENHAVEN PRESS
An imprint of Thomson Gale, a part of The Thomson Corporation

Fitchburg Public Library
5530 Lacy Road
Fitchburg, WI 53711

THOMSON
GALE

Detroit • New York • San Francisco • New Haven, Conn. • Waterville, Maine • London

Christine Nasso, *Publisher*
Elizabeth Des Chenes, *Managing Editor*

© 2008 The Gale Group.

Star logo is a trademark and Gale and Greenhaven Press are registered trademarks used herein under license.

For more information, contact:
Greenhaven Press
27500 Drake Rd.
Farmington Hills, MI 48331-3535
Or you can visit our Internet site at http://www.gale.com

ALL RIGHTS RESERVED
No part of this work covered by the copyright hereon may be reproduced or used in any form or by any means—graphic, electronic, or mechanical, including photocopying, recording, taping, Web distribution, or information storage retrieval systems—without the written permission of the publisher.

Articles in Greenhaven Press anthologies are often edited for length to meet page requirements. In addition, original titles of these works are changed to clearly present the main thesis and to explicitly indicate the author's opinion. Every effort is made to ensure that Greenhaven Press accurately reflects the original intent of the authors. Every effort has been made to trace the owners of copyrighted material.

Cover photograph reproduced by permission of Gstar.

LIBRARY OF CONGRESS CATALOGING-IN-PUBLICATION DATA

School Violence / Lucinda Almond, book editor.
p. cm. -- (Current controversies)
Includes bibliographical references and index.
ISBN-13: 978-0-7377-3795-0 (hardcover)
ISBN-13: 978-0-7377-3796-7 (pbk.)
1. School violence--United States. I. Almond, Lucinda.
LB3013.32.S3763 2008
371.7'820973--dc22

2007029879

ISBN-10: 0-7377-3795-6 (hardcover)
ISBN-10: 0-7377-3796-4 (pbk.)

Printed in the United States of America
10 9 8 7 6 5 4 3 2 1

Contents

Chapter 2: What Factors Contribute to School Violence?

Foreword

By definition, controversies are "discussions of questions in which opposing opinions clash" (Webster's Twentieth Century Dictionary Unabridged). Few would deny that controversies are a pervasive part of the human condition and exist on virtually every level of human enterprise. Controversies transpire between individuals and among groups, within nations and between nations. Controversies supply the grist necessary for progress by providing challenges and challengers to the status quo. They also create atmospheres where strife and warfare can flourish. A world without controversies would be a peaceful world; but it also would be, by and large, static and prosaic.

The Series' Purpose

The purpose of the Current Controversies series is to explore many of the social, political, and economic controversies dominating the national and international scenes today. Titles selected for inclusion in the series are highly focused and specific. For example, from the larger category of criminal justice, Current Controversies deals with specific topics such as police brutality, gun control, white collar crime, and others. The debates in Current Controversies also are presented in a useful, timeless fashion. Articles and book excerpts included in each title are selected if they contribute valuable, long-range ideas to the overall debate. And wherever possible, current information is enhanced with historical documents and other relevant materials. Thus, while individual titles are current in focus, every effort is made to ensure that they will not become quickly outdated. Books in the Current Controversies series will remain important resources for librarians, teachers, and students for many years.

In addition to keeping the titles focused and specific, great care is taken in the editorial format of each book in the series. Book introductions and chapter prefaces are offered to provide background material for readers. Chapters are organized around several key questions that are answered with diverse opinions representing all points on the political spectrum. Materials in each chapter include opinions in which authors clearly disagree as well as alternative opinions in which authors may agree on a broader issue but disagree on the possible solutions. In this way, the content of each volume in Current Controversies mirrors the mosaic of opinions encountered in society. Readers will quickly realize that there are many viable answers to these complex issues. By questioning each author's conclusions, students and casual readers can begin to develop the critical thinking skills so important to evaluating opinionated material.

Current Controversies is also ideal for controlled research. Each anthology in the series is composed of primary sources taken from a wide gamut of informational categories including periodicals, newspapers, books, U.S. and foreign government documents, and the publications of private and public organizations. Readers will find factual support for reports, debates, and research papers covering all areas of important issues. In addition, an annotated table of contents, an index, a book and periodical bibliography, and a list of organizations to contact are included in each book to expedite further research.

Perhaps more than ever before in history, people are confronted with diverse and contradictory information. During the Persian Gulf War, for example, the public was not only treated to minute-to-minute coverage of the war, it was also inundated with critiques of the coverage and countless analyses of the factors motivating U.S. involvement. Being able to sort through the plethora of opinions accompanying today's major issues, and to draw one's own conclusions, can be a complicated and frustrating struggle. It is the editors' hope that Current Controversies will help readers with this struggle.

Introduction

The Virginia Tech Massacre was a school shooting that took place on April 16, 2007, at Virginia Polytechnic Institute and State University in Blacksburg, Virginia. Seung-Hui Cho, a twenty-three-year-old student, killed thirty-two people and injured twenty-nine before committing suicide, making it the deadliest mass murder in U.S. history. Cho had a history of problems at the school, including allegations of stalking, referrals to counseling, and a 2005 declaration of mental illness by a Virginia court. Cho's emotional detachment was evident through his middle and high school years, during which time he was bullied for speech difficulties. "Relatives thought he might be a mute. Or mentally ill," reported the *New York Times*. Police found a suicide note in Cho's dorm room, which included comments about "rich kids," "debauchery," and "deceitful charlatans" on campus. Cho's grandfather was quoted in the *Daily Mirror*, referring to Cho as a person who deserved to die with the victims. On April 20, Cho's family issued a statement of grief and apology, written by his sister, Sun-Kyung Cho.

This massacre revived the gun control debate in the United States. Proponents of gun control argued that guns are too accessible, citing that Cho, a mentally disturbed person, was able to purchase two semiautomatic pistols. Proponents of gun rights argued that Virginia Tech's gun-free "safe zone" policy ensured that none of the students or faculty would be armed, guaranteeing that no one could stop Cho's rampage. Others argued for closing loopholes in the laws that would prevent people like Cho from purchasing guns, while at the same time protecting citizens' rights to own guns.

Experts across various fields maintain that violent movies and video games, poverty, bullying, single-parent families, lack of mental health services, and out-of-control kids all contribute to the school "killing fields" landscape. Most of these violent offenders do not wake up one morning and decide to kill; rather, they plan, plot, and acquire weapons in a methodical manner that will ensure destruction. Teens who carry out these evil rampages often complain of being angry with the world; they feel mistreated and want to "right" all the "wrongs" that have been inflicted upon them. These feelings have always existed throughout history, so why is there a sudden surge of school violence and killings?

Some argue that the juvenile justice system itself mishandles teens who are in need of social services—not punitive measures—thereby exacerbating the problem by locking them up with other teens with similar problems. This setting gives teens an opportunity to share angry feelings and encourage one another to participate in vindictive, violent behaviors. David M. Altschuler, a Johns Hopkins University criminologist and nationally known expert on juvenile justice, believes that kids should not be institutionalized and then released back into the same neighborhood, family, or circle of friends. Altschuler claims that if people knew just how poor and unsafe juvenile correction facilities were, they would not favor incarceration. Instead, he argues, society could better serve teens by providing group homes and day program settings that provide job skills, techniques for anger management, conflict resolution, and behavior modification. Altschuler contends that rehabilitation, not punishment, should be society's goal.

Not everyone, however, is eager to accept nurturing philosophies when it comes to violent teens. Michael Paranzino, who runs an advocacy group called Throw Away the Key, says that "public safety is the main goal of incarceration—for adult offenders and juveniles." With respect to juvenile justice, Paranzino believes that so-called experts have little or no concern for the innocent people in society. "If teenagers can't live their lives without harming other people, they should be separated from other people."

Regardless of the disputes among experts, society has an urgent need to understand why teens kill. Their crimes often seem senseless and random, and a need for an explanation is always foremost in people's minds. Helen Smith, MD, a forensic psychologist, believes that society will buy into just about any type of explanation, such as violent movies or computer games, because their need for an answer is satisfied. These reasons may provide temporary comfort, but they distract from the real reason. Dr. Smith argues that the explanation is much more simple and obvious. She contends that teens become killers because they are mentally disturbed individuals who are pushed over the edge by seemingly innocuous events or influences. She points out that Charles Manson, a mass-murder ringleader from the 1960s, claimed to find inspiration for his crimes in a Beatles song. Dr. Smith points to those individuals who are drug users, have below-average intelligence, and a history of cruelty to animals or siblings as prime candidates to become killers. Teens who kill also believe that others do not have any rights. That is what makes it so easy for them to unleash their frustration and rage on innocent people. However, the most important reason why teens commit murder is because the social safeguards that used to be in place no longer exist, or are failing. Dr. Smith states that, "families, churches, school, child welfare authorities, courts . . . are all becoming less and less effective at keeping these potential killers from reaching their final, lethal stage."

In any event, most courts continue to treat violent teens as children; their status as a criminal is secondary to their age. However, according to the U.S. Department of Justice, crimes committed by youths have increased by 60 percent since 1984. Since 1965, the number of twelve-year-olds arrested for violent crimes has doubled, and the number of thirteen and fourteen-year-olds has tripled. The seriousness of their crimes has increased, as well. Truancy and vandalism have been replaced with more violent crimes such as arson, rape, and murder.

These far-reaching events cry out for a solution. The authors of *Current Controversies: School Violence* debate the causes of school violence and seek a better understanding of effective preventive measures that will eliminate the tragedies that some teens inflict on others. The authors' beliefs and proposed solutions vary greatly, but they all share a common goal of securing safe schools for all students.

Chapter 1

Is School Violence a Prevalent Problem?

Chapter Preface

The Guns-Free Act of 1994 requires that all schools automatically expel students who bring firearms onto school property. That law has now morphed into a zero-tolerance disciplinary policy adopted by most schools, which allows for expulsions for fighting, disobedience, and disruptive behavior. Some schools circumvent the principal's office altogether when there is a behavioral problem; instead, the police are notified and the student is arrested, even at elementary schools. What were once considered childhood pranks or normal kid behavior can now result in jail time.

When Jerry, an eight-year-old student in Espanola, New Mexico, refused to return to class while he was still crying over a disciplinary action with a counselor, the counselor called the police to confine him "until (he) changes his attitude."

In Monticello, Florida, seven-year-old Johnnie was arrested for hitting and scratching a classmate and teacher.

In St. Petersburg, Florida, a five-year-old girl was arrested for disobedience, including kicking a teacher and breaking a candy dish. This forty-pound young girl was handcuffed with plastic ties; her ankles were chained with handcuffs.

In Visalia, California, eleven-year-old Tate—a second-place winner in his school's science fair—spent six hours in jail after he threatened a menacing classmate with a pencil. Principal Rosemary Spencer said, "We had to do something or we could've had another Columbine or what happened in Minnesota [school shootings] on our hands."

If these seemingly innocuous events are included in the nationwide statistics for school violence, then are the statistics truly reflective of the problems on campuses? Joel Best, professor of sociology and criminal justice at the University of Delaware, cautions against accepting these numbers without critical analysis. Most people assume that numbers are factual, and when the statistics are combined with dramatic, headline-grabbing incidents, they create the impression that school violence is on the rise. For instance, former CBS anchor Dan Rather reported that "school shootings in this country have become an epidemic."

"Such claims have become commonplace among journalists who haven't thought carefully enough about the evidence," says Best.

The validity of and reliance on statistics is often the focus of debates concerning the prevalence of school violence. Experts on either side of the debate may have equally impressive studies and statistics, yet their conclusions and recommendations contradict one another. School violence discussions vary in scope and content; often, hostile accusations of political or personal agendas are hurled at those who conduct the study or those who support the study. Some schools downplay their violence problems in order to avoid penalties from the government; others may exaggerate their problems in order to receive more government funds.

There are even disputes concerning the meaning of the words "school violence." Many people conjure up images of shootings or stabbings on campus, while others imagine a fight between twelve-year-old boys. The National Criminal Justice Reference Service recognizes violence as "any behavior that violates a school's educational mission or climate of respect or jeopardizes the intent of the school to be free of aggression against persons or property, drugs, weapons, disruptions, and disorder." This definition captures the idea that school violence takes many forms and is not limited to the most hostile acts. It also takes into account precursor behaviors that lead up to more violent behaviors. According to the North Carolina Department of Juvenile Justice and Delinquency Prevention (NCDJJDP), these behaviors include put-downs, insults, threats, trash talk, bullying, and pushing. The

NCDJJDP states that "as one advances from one type of behavior to the next, the level of violence increases with fighting, sexual harassment, stealing, drinking and drugs, weapons, vandalism, hate crimes, gangs, hostages, rape, murder, and suicide completing the continuum. What all of this really means is that efforts which are directed at school violence prevention must focus on a broader definition and understanding of what constitutes school violence. Trying to prevent school violence only in terms of physical security measures which are designed to keep guns and other weapons out of schools is not enough."

The prevalence and scope of school violence continues to be debated. The authors in the following chapter present their arguments concerning the state of school safety, teens who are in need of intervention, and the media's role in shaping the public's perception of school violence.

Schools Underreport Incidences of School Violence

Alan G. Hevesi

Alan G. Hevesi is a former New York State assemblyman and comptroller.

Violent incidents in New York State high schools have not been accurately reported to the State Education Department (SED) and SED has not done enough to address misreporting problem or to effectively identify schools with serious violence problems, according to an audit released . . . [on May 22, 2006] by Comptroller Alan G. Hevesi.

School districts around the state are required to submit data regarding violent and disruptive incidents to SED under the Safe Schools Against Violence in Education (SAVE) Act, which went into effect in 2000. SED is required to review the information to determine if any schools should be designated as persistently dangerous, and to publish an annual list of the state's most dangerous schools.

"We simply cannot ignore the fact that violence is occurring in schools in urban, suburban and rural settings all around the state. It is essential to get information about this problem so that we can work to make our schools safer for all children and to direct young people who are involved in violence toward productive and law-abiding adulthood," Hevesi said. "However, SED is failing to manage the school violence reporting program effectively, and some school districts are not reporting accurate information. As a result, it is harder to accurately determine where and what kinds of resources need to be provided to help prevent school violence."

Alan G. Hevesi, "Audit: SED Mismanaging School Violence Data Collection, Some Schools Underreporting Violent Incidents," *News from the Office of the New York State Comptroller*, May 22, 2006. www.osc.state.ny.us. Reproduced by permission.

Up to 93 Percent of Incidences Are Not Reported

Auditors visited 15 school districts to review the records kept by school officials to track violent incidents and compare the school data to what was actually reported to SED. The audit includes detailed data from each of these school districts. The districts visited were: Adirondack (Oneida County), Albany (Albany), Ardsley (Westchester), Brentwood (Suffolk), Hempstead (Nassau), Hudson (Columbia), Niagara Falls (Niagara), Plattsburgh (Clinton), Rochester (Monroe), Saratoga (Saratoga), Schenectady (Schenectady), Syracuse (Onondaga), Uniondale (Nassau), Waterville (Oneida) and White Plains (Westchester). Auditors also spoke with officials at 35 additional school districts regarding the reporting process.

Ten of 17 schools . . . failed to report at least one incident in which a weapon was used or possessed.

At ten of the 15 school districts visited, auditors found that at least one-third of violent incidents documented in school records were not reported to SED. At five of the school districts, more than eight out of ten incidents were not reported to SED.

Albany High School, for example, reported 144 incidents to SED for the 2003–2004 school year, but auditors found that records at the school indicated that 924 incidents had actually occurred, which meant that 84 percent (780) of the incidents were not reported. The incidents not reported to SED included:

- 106 assaults with physical injury including four involving the use of a weapon;
- 55 instances of intimidation, harassment, menacing or bullying;

- 14 burglaries or thefts;
- Two sexual offenses; and
- One bomb threat.

White Plains High School reported 22 violent and disruptive incidents during the same year. Auditors found that school records actually detailed 311 occurrences, which meant that 93 percent (289) were not reported, including:

- 35 assaults with physical injury;
- 23 instances of intimidation, harassment, menacing or bullying;
- One sexual offense; and
- 181 other disruptive incidents.

SED maintained that the materials were understandable, and suggested that schools used confusion as an excuse for not making full and accurate reports.

Auditors also found:

- Ardsley High School failed to report 100 of 106 incidents, or 94 percent.
- Hudson High School failed to report 266 of 282 documented incidents, or 94 percent.
- Niagara Falls High School failed to report 553 of 624 incidents, or 89 percent.

School Administrators Manipulate the Data

Many of the most serious incidents were not reported to SED. Ten of 17 schools at the 15 districts for which records were reviewed failed to report at least one incident in which a weapon was used or possessed. Three of these schools—Schenectady

(21 incidents with weapons), Ardsley (4 incidents) and Waterville (2 incidents) failed to report any such incidents in this category. At Charlotte High School in Rochester, 31 of 39 incidents with weapons (80 percent) went unreported to SED.

Officials at nearly two-thirds of the districts contacted told auditors that the explanatory materials provided by SED relating to filing the data on violent incidents were unclear and confusing. School officials reported that the incident categories were vague and did not cover all possible occurrences. SED maintained that the materials were understandable, and suggested that schools used confusion as an excuse for not making full and accurate reports.

After significant reporting problems in the first two years of the program, SED took several steps including modification of the standardized reporting form, providing more detailed instructions and conducting training sessions for school officials. However, SED did not have any record of which schools attended these sessions, and school officials who did attend said that conflicting information was presented at different sessions. Auditors also found errors in incident data after it was entered in SED's database, and determined that controls over data processing at SED were not adequate.

There is a huge loophole in the system for some of the most dangerous schools.

To determine whether a school will be classified as "persistently dangerous," SED assigns a numerical violence index score to each school based on the number and seriousness of the incidents and the enrollment of the school. If a school's violence index is 25 or higher for two years in a row, it is placed on the preliminary list of persistently dangerous schools. The designated school then has the opportunity to challenge the classification, and may submit revised data.

Auditors noted that SED does not require schools to provide documentation to support any revised data that is submitted. Furthermore, SED provides schools on the preliminary list with a detailed description of how the violence index is calculated—information that is not otherwise made available to schools that are not on the list. As a result, auditors found "strong indications" that incident data was manipulated, since schools knew precisely what revised data to submit to bring down their violence index and thereby be removed from the list of persistently dangerous schools.

In fact, of 21 schools on the preliminary list in 2003–04, three closed and 14 of the remaining 18 were removed from the list in 2005.

Students and Parents Deserve Meaningful Data

"SED needs to exert strong leadership to make the information collected regarding violent incidents more accurate and meaningful. Instead, there is a huge loophole in the system for some of the most dangerous schools," Hevesi said. "SED is letting down parents and children—and New York's taxpayers."

Under the SAVE legislation, the parents of children attending schools designated as persistently dangerous must be given the option of sending their children to another school in the district, if one is available. A similar option is also required under the federal No Child Left Behind Act. Because of the questions raised about the accuracy of SED's data regarding violent incidents, auditors noted that parents who should have the option may not get it.

Technology Provides New Forms of Bullying

Justin W. Patchin and Sameer Hinduja

Justin W. Patchin is an assistant professor of criminal justice at the University of Wisconsin. Sameer Hinduja is an assistant professor in the department of criminology and criminal justice at Florida Atlantic University.

The home, neighborhood, and school are all recognized as important social and physical contexts within which adolescents develop. Bullying—an all too common form of youthful violence—has historically affected children and teenagers only while at school, while traveling to or from school, or in public places such as playgrounds and bus stops. Modern technology, however, has enabled would-be bullies to extend the reach of their aggression and threats beyond this physical setting through what can be termed *cyberbullying*, where tech-savvy students are able to harass others day and night using technological devices such as computer systems and cellular phones. . . .

Bullying Can Be Violent and Destructive

Little research to date has been conducted on cyberbulling. However, research on the correlates of traditional bullying can assist in comprehending the reality and growth of this new phenomenon. To begin, the desire to be and remain popular takes on almost life-like proportions among kids and teenagers during certain stages of their life, and their self-esteem is largely defined by the way that others view them. Although it is unclear exactly when self-esteem increases or decreases dur-

Justin W. Patchin and Sameer Hinduja, "Bullies Move Beyond the Schoolyard: A Preliminary Look at Cyberbullying," *Youth Violence and Juvenile Justice*, vol. 4, no. 2, April 2006, pp. 148–156, 158, 162, 164. Copyright © 2006 by Sage Publications. Reproduced by permission of Sage Publications, Inc.

ing a child's life, it unquestionably shapes a child's development in profound ways. According to the social acceptance model, self-esteem stems from the perceptions that others have of the individual. When individuals perceive themselves to be rejected or otherwise socially excluded, a number of ill effects can result. Much research has validated this theory and has pointed to the following potentially negative outcomes: depression, substance abuse, and aggression. In addition, low self-esteem tends to be found among chronic victims of traditional bullying. It is expected that cyberbullying can similarly cripple the self-esteem of a child or adolescent, and without a support system or prosocial outlets through which to resolve and mitigate the strain, the same dysphoric and maladaptive outcomes may result. . . .

Although the harassment associated with bullying can occur anywhere, the term *bullying* often denotes the behavior as it occurs among youth in school hallways and bathrooms, on the playground, or otherwise proximal or internal to the school setting. Bullies can also follow their prey to other venues such as malls, restaurants, or neighborhood hangouts to continue the harassment. In the past, interaction in a physical context was required for victimization to occur. This is no longer the case thanks to the increased prevalence of the Internet, personal computers, and cellular phones. Now, would-be bullies are afforded technology that provides additional mediums over which they can manifest their malice. . . .

Prevalence and Consequences of Bullying

It is unclear exactly how many youth are bullied or bully others on any given day. In 1982, 49 fifth grade teachers from Cleveland, Ohio, reported that almost one fourth (23%) of their 1,078 students were either victims or bullies. More recently [2001] a nationally representative study of 15,686 students in grades 6 through 10 identified that approximately 11% of respondents were victims of bullying, 13% were bullies, and 6% were both victims and bullies during a year. Additional research conducted by the Family Work Institute substantiated these findings through interviews with 1,000 youth in grades 5 through 12. Their study [in 2002] found that 12% of youth were bullied five or more times during the previous month. Finally, the Bureau of Justice Statistics reports [in 2002] that 8% of youth between the ages of 12 and 18 had been victims of bullying in the previous 6 months. That said, conservative estimates maintain that at least 5% of those in primary and secondary schools (ages 7–16) are victimized by bullies each day.

Physical separation of the bully and the victim is no longer a limitation in the frequency, scope and depth of harm experienced and doled out.

Many young people are able to shrug off instances of being bullied, perhaps because of peer or familial support or higher self-efficacy. Nonetheless, others are not able to cope in a prosocial or normative manner or reconcile the pain experienced through more serious episodes or actions. Suicidal ideation, eating disorders, and chronic illness have beset many of those who have have been tormented by bullies, whereas other victims run away from home. In addition, depression has been a frequently cited consequence of bullying and seems to perpetuate into adulthood, evidencing the potentially long-term implications of mistreatment during adolescence. Finally, in extreme cases, victims have responded with extreme violence such as physical assault, homicide, and suicide. . . .

Aspects of High-Tech Bullying

Because of the advent and continued growth of technological advances, the transmutation of bullying has occurred—from the physical to the virtual. Physical separation of the bully and the victim is no longer a limitation in the frequency, scope, and depth of harm experienced and doled out. As instances of bullying are no longer restricted to real-world settings, the problem has matured. Although a migration to the electronic realm is a seemingly logical extension for bullies, little is currently known regarding the nature and extent of the phenomenon. In short, we define *cyberbullying* as willful and repeated harm inflicted through the medium of electronic text. Based on the literature reviewed above, the constructs of malicious intent, violence, repetition, and power differential appear most salient when constructing a comprehensive definition of traditional bullying and are similarly appropriate when attempting to define this new permutation. To be sure, cyberbullies are malicious aggressors who seek implicit or explicit pleasure or profit through the mistreatment of other individuals. Violence is often associated with aggression and corresponds to actions intended to inflict injury (of any type). One instance of mistreatment, although potentially destructive, cannot accurately be equated to bullying, and so cyberbullying must also involve harmful behavior of a repetitive nature. Finally, because of the very nature of the behavior, cyberbullies have some perceived or actual power over their victims. Although power in traditional bullying might be physical (stature) or social (competency or popularity), online power may simply stem from proficiency. That is, youth who are able to navigate the electronic world and utilize technology in a way that allows them to harass others are in a power relative to victim. . . .

There are two major electronic devices that young bullies can employ to harass their victim from afar. First, using a personal computer, a bully can send harassing e-mails or instant messages, post obscene, insulting, and slanderous messages to online bulletin boards, or develop Web sites to promote and disseminate defamatory content. Second, harassing text messages can be sent to the victim via cellular phones. . . .

Issues Specific to Cyberbullying

Jean (French sociologist) Gabriel Tarde's (1903) law of insertion suggests that new technologies will be applied to augment traditional activities and behaviors. Certain characteristics inherent in these technologies increase the likelihood that they will be exploited for deviant purposes. Cellular phones and personal computers offer several advantages to individuals inclined to harass others. First, electronic bullies can remain virtually anonymous. Temporary e-mail accounts and pseudonyms in chat rooms, instant messaging programs, and other Internet venues can make it very difficult for adolescents to determine the identity of aggressors. Individuals can hide behind some measure of anonymity when using their personal computer or cellular phone to bully another individual, which perhaps frees them from normative and social constraints on their behavior. Further, it seems that bullies might be emboldened when using electronic means to effectuate their antagonistic agenda because it takes less energy and fortitude to express hurtful comments using a keyboard or keypad than using one's voice.

There may truly be no rest for the weary as cyberbullying penetrates the walls of a home, traditionally a place where victims could seek refuge.

Second, supervision is lacking in cyberspace. Although chat hosts regularly observe the dialogue in some chat rooms in an effort to police conversations and evict offensive individuals, personal messages sent between users are viewable only by the sender and the recipient and are therefore outside regulatory reach. Furthermore, there are no individuals to monitor or censor offensive content in e-mail or text messages sent via computer or cellular phone. Another contributive element is the increasingly common presence of computers in the private environments of adolescent bedrooms. Indeed, teenagers often know more about computers and cellular phones than do their parents and are therefore able to operate the technologies without worry or concern that a probing parent will discover their participation in bullying (or even their victimization).

In a similar vein, the inseparability of a cellular phone from its owner makes that person a perpetual target for victimization. Users often need to keep it turned on for legitimate uses, which provides the opportunity for those with malicious intentions to send threatening and insulting statements via the cellular phone's text messaging capabilities. There may truly be no rest for the weary as cyberbullying penetrates the walls of a home, traditionally a place where victims could seek refuge.

Finally, electronic devices allow individuals to contact others (both for prosocial and antisocial purposes) at all times and in almost all places. The fact that most adolescents (83%) connect to the Internet from home indicates that online bullying can be an invasive phenomenon that can hound a person even when not at or around school. Relatedly, the coordination of a bullying attack can occur with more ease because it is not constrained by the physical location of the bullies or victims. A veritable onslaught of mistreatment can quickly and effectively torment a victim through the use of these communications and connectivity tools.

Bullying in Any Form Causes Emotional Turmoil

Of course, cyberbullying is a problem only to the extent that it produces harm toward the victim. In the traditional sense, a victim is often under the immediate threat of violence and physical harm and also subject to humiliation and embarrassment in a public setting. These elements compound the already serious psychological, emotional, and social wounds inflicted through such mistreatment. One might argue that a victim of bullying in cyberspace—whether via e-mail, instant messaging, or cellular phone text messaging—can quickly escape from the harassment by deleting the e-mail, closing the instant message, and shutting off the cellular phone and is largely protected from overt acts of violence by the offender through geographic and spatial distance. Such an argument holds much truth; however, the fact remains that if social acceptance is crucially important to a youth's identity and self-esteem, cyberbullying can capably and perhaps more permanently wreak psychological, emotional, and social havoc. It is not a stretch to say that physical harm—such as being beaten up—might even be preferred by some victims to the excruciating pain they experience from nonphysical harm because the former can heal quicker. Furthermore, it is yet to be determined if there is a causal pathway between cyberbullying and traditional bullying, and so physical harm might very well follow as a logical outcome of a continually increasing desire on the part of the offender to most severely hurt the victim. To be sure, this must be explored in future studies....

Almost 30% of the adolescent respondents reported that they had been victims of online bullying.

Because of the widespread availability of electronic devices, there is no lack of participants using the technologies. Their ubiquity provides a seemingly endless pool of candidates who are susceptible to being bullied or to becoming a bully. Unfortunately, however, little is known in terms of how often these technologies are mobilized for deviant purposes. One empirical study has been conducted to date: In 2002, the National Children's Home—a charitable organization in London—surveyed 856 youth between the ages of 11 and 19 and found that 16% received threatening text messages via their cellular phone, 7% had been bullied in online chat rooms, and 4% had been harassed via e-mail. Following the victimization, 42% told a friend, 32% told a parent or guardian, and 29% did not reveal the experience to anyone....

Analysis of Cyberbullying

The current study involved an analysis of youthful Internet users in an effort to assess their perceptions of, and experiences with, electronic bullying. It is difficult to individually observe the nature and extent of electronic bullying among adolescent Internet users because of the "private" nature of e-mails, cellular phone text messages, and instant messages and one-on-one chat messages within online chat channels. To be sure, if the instances of cyberbullying occur in a public forum such as a popular chat channel and in the view of all chat room members, then direct observation and consequent analyses may be possible. Most of the time, however, they occur through private (nonpublic), person-to-person communications. A survey methodology was therefore designed to collect data by requiring participants to recall and relate their cyberbullying practices and experiences via a questionnaire that was linked from the official Web site of a popular music artist revered by the target age group. An electronic format was selected as it allows for efficiency in collecting data from a large number of participants. The survey was active between May 1, 2004, and May 31, 2004. . . .

Because this was an Internet-based survey, anyone could participate. Even though the survey was associated with a teen-oriented Web site, individuals from all ages also frequent the site and therefore completed the survey. . . . Out of the 571 total respondents, 384 were younger than 18 (67.3%; henceforth referred to as the *youth sample*). In both groups, the vast majority of respondents were female. This finding is likely attributable to the nature of the Web site on which the survey was linked (a female pop music star). . . .

Adult Intervention Is Needed

The results of this study point to a number of key issues. First, bullying is occurring online and is impacting youth in many negative ways. Almost 30% of the adolescent respondents reported that they had been victims of online bullying—operationalized as having been ignored, disrespected, called names, threatened, picked on, or made fun of or having had rumors spread by others. Admittedly, being ignored by another person may simply reflect obnoxious behavior that warranted the outcome rather than actual and willful aggression. We were not able to parcel out the stimuli of instances when people were ignored but chose to include a measure of it in the current analyses. This is because universal social acceptance is still largely desired by children and adolescents, even if as adults we understand that it is impossible to please everyone at all times. Being ignored would introduce dissonance and instability to the already tenuous relational and social equilibria sought by youths and may accordingly be considered a passive-aggressive form of bullying. Along similar lines, although some of this harassment may be characterized as trivial (e.g., being ignored by others or being disrespected), more than 20% reported being threatened by others. Anger and frustration was a commonly reported emotional response to the harassment. Finally, almost 60% of victims were affected by the online behaviors at school, at home, or with friends.

Several policy implications stem from the aforementioned findings. It is hoped that this harmful phenomena can be curtailed by proactively addressing the potentially negative uses of technology. Parents must regularly monitor the activities in which their children are engaged while online. Teachers, too, must take care to supervise students as they use computers in the classrooms. Police officers must investigate those instances of cyberbullying that are potentially injurious and hold responsible parties accountable. Unfortunately, there are no methods to discern which harassment involves simple jest and which has the potential to escalate into serious violence. Future research must analyze case studies and anecdotal stories of cyberbullying experiences to help determine when intervention by authority figures is most appropriate. Overall, parents, teachers, police officers, and other community leaders must keep up with technological advances so that they are equipped with the tools and knowledge to identify and address any problems when they arise. . . .

More Research Is Needed

The preceding review provides a description of bullying in cyberspace for the purposes of introducing it as a topic meriting academic inquiry and underscoring its often inescapable pernicious nature. Indeed, 74% of the youth in this study reported that bullying occurs online, and almost 30% of the youth reported being victimized by others while online. Some may dismiss electronic bullying as normative behavior that does not physically harm anyone. To be sure, some have this perception regarding traditional bullying, dismissing it as a rite of passage or an inevitable and even instructive element of growing up. Because of the familiarity and memorability of bullying as almost unavoidable in both the schoolyard and neighborhood milieu during one's formative years, perhaps the reader may share those sentiments.

Because no consensus exists when considering whether cyberbullying merits increased attention because of society's continued progression into a wired world, perhaps it should just be considered another contemporary cultural challenge that kids often face when transitioning into adulthood. Conceivably there is no need to panic when introduced to the concept that online bullying does and will continue to take place as children seek to carve out an identity for themselves and cope with various pressures associated with their development. Alternatively, perhaps there is a need for alarm as both those who bully and those who are bullied might yield readily to other criminogenic influences and proceed down a path of deviance online, offline, or both. Regardless, cyberbullying is very real, and it is hoped that this work has highlighted its relevance for the purposes of inspiring additional interest in its etiology and consequences.

Youths Are Angry and Out of Control

Sandra P. Thomas

Sandra P. Thomas is a professor and director of the PhD Nursing Program, College of Nursing, at the University of Tennessee at Knoxville.

Youth violence is a serious problem in America, commanding attention from school officials, behavioral science researchers, and juvenile justice personnel. Although recent reports suggest some decline in juvenile arrests for Violent Crime Index (VCI) offenses, . . . fewer than half of violent crimes by young people are ever reported to the police. Even if arrests for VCI offenses such as aggravated assault and murder are decreasing, studies show U.S. school children remain heavily involved in fighting, weapon carrying, and bullying (which can include both psychological and physical abuse). In the national priorities outlined in *Healthy People 2010* (U.S. Department of Health and Human Services, 2000), reduction of adolescent physical fighting and weapon carrying to school are specific objectives.

Teen Anger Is Out of Control

Out-of-control anger behavior appears to be rampant among youth, perhaps echoing the behavior modeled by adults who engage in road rage, air rage, and desk rage. A recent [2001] survey of more than 15,000 teenagers showed that 75% of boys and more than 60% of girls had hit someone in the past 12 months because they were angry. The high frequency of bullying behavior has been documented in several studies.

Sandra P. Thomas, "School Connectedness, Anger Behaviors, and Relationships of Violent and Nonviolent American Youth," *Perspectives in Psychiatric Care*, October–December 2004. Copyright © 2004 Basil Blackwell Ltd. Reproduced by permission of Blackwell Publishers.

More than 1 in 6 sixth- to tenth-graders say they are bullied sometimes; more than 1 in 12 say they are bullied once per week or more. In an online poll conducted by Time for Kids [2001], 27% of the respondents admitted bullying others, and 41% said they had been picked on. Middle-school students . . . reported being teased and bullied about their physical appearance, personality and behavior, family and environment, and school-related factors such as academic ability. "Being different in any way" was the underlying theme in focus-group discussions with these students.

Teasing and bullying escalated when students were highly sensitive, cried, or acted "odd." The bystanding audience often supports bullying behavior, as shown in a study of more than 10,000 third- to ninth-graders; 10% to 20% experienced a vicarious thrill from watching other students being bullied.

The school shooters were social outcasts who had experienced bullying and other forms of cruel treatment from classmates.

Weapons are prevalent on school property despite metal detectors and other security measures. National data from the Centers for Disease Control and Prevention (CDC, 1999) showed that more than 1 in 13 students were threatened or injured with a weapon (such as a gun, knife, or club) on school property in the past year. Josephson Institute data (2001) revealed that more than 1 in 5 (21%) high-school boys and 15% of middle-school boys took a weapon to school at least once during the past year. Nearly 1 in 3 middle-school boys (31%) and 60% of high-school boys said they could get a gun if they wanted to. . . .

Risk Factors for Youth Violence

While the etiology of youth violence is complex, many risk factors are well known, including family factors such as parental criminality, child maltreatment, and low levels of parental involvement. The predictive power of factors such as poverty, residence in a violent community, and neighborhood disorganization is also well established. But the massacre at Columbine, perpetrated by boys from an affluent community, defied explanation in terms of these established risk factors, many of which were absent from the profile of the Columbine shooters. Instead, school-related factors appeared more salient. The school shooters were social outcasts who had experienced bullying and other forms of cruel treatment from classmates. . . .

Researchers have found a direct relationship between school disconnectedness and outcomes such as delinquency, truancy, drug use, and a number of physical and mental health indicators. Students who feel close to others, fairly treated, and vested in school are less likely to engage in risky behaviors than those who do not. Harsh disciplinary policies (e.g., expulsion for a first offense) produce lower school connectedness. Greater connectedness is promoted by a climate of positive classroom management, smaller school size, and higher student participation in extracurricular activities. This line of research is important because school connectedness is a modifiable factor: Poverty, community disorganization, and family neglect are not. . . .

Gender and Racial Differences in Anger and School Connectedness

Some gender and racial differences in anger have been discovered in previous research. For example, boys and girls are aroused to anger by different sorts of provocations. To a female, the most anger-provoking behavior of another person is an accusation of being promiscuous; to a male, it is the accusation of being cowardly. . . . Girls were angry because of interpersonal experiences, and directed their anger inwardly; boys were angry in situations in which their performance was evaluated, and directed the anger outwardly. . . . These differences are attributable to traditional gender role socialization in which boys are encouraged to be tough and physical, whereas girls are encouraged to be passive and indirect. . . .

Ethnic/racial differences in anger and violent behavior of young people deserve closer attention, because studies are few. . . . [One study] found Mexican-American middle and high school students less likely than whites to be verbally aggressive when angry. Black elementary students, whether male or female, had greater general propensity to be angry (trait anger) and higher anger-out scores than whites. . . . Whites scored higher on anger reflection/control (resolving conflict via a cognitive approach). In an adolescent sample of African, Hispanic, and European Americans, trait anger was higher in African Americans. . . . Hispanic students scored lower on outwardly expressed anger.

Findings of the study suggest that interventions are needed to increase the social competence and connectedness of alienated students.

Little information is available to date about school connectedness in students with different racial characteristics. It is reasonable to hypothesize, however, that minority students may feel less affinity for school. There is growing evidence that black students are more severely disciplined than whites and 2.4 times more likely to be suspended. Furthermore, black students are often disciplined for "nebulous infractions" such as being too noisy. Black race was associated with lower school connectedness in a study of 1,959 seventh- to twelfth-graders at eight public schools. Blacks (and females) felt less connected to school in an analysis. . . on more than 75,000 students in 127 schools. . . .

Students Feel Victimized and Angry

Qualitative data, gleaned from responses to the open-ended questions of . . . [our] survey, were subjected to content analysis. We present here only the findings pertinent to school connectedness. The students resented (a) schools' emphasis on surveillance, conformity, and regimentation; (b) schools' inequitable discipline of "jocks" and other high-status groups versus the rest of the student body; (c) schools' overreaction to trivial offenses; and (d) schools' lack of action when they report bullying and harassment. These are just a few of the student comments:

Schools' emphasis on surveillance, conformity, and regimentation:

- You can't be you. You have to dress a certain way, walk in a line, don't talk, put your hand up, do this, don't do that. But they teach you to be you.
- There have been times when I felt that the teachers were biased against me during grading just because of the way I dress.
- Students are forced to conform to the school's way of learning. Any attempt to approach assignments differently is immediately shot down verbally or in the grading process. . . .

Schools' inequitable discipline:

- The school needs jocks, so they never get punished and are allowed to treat everyone else like trash. The preps can have their mommies' and daddies' lawyers make sure they never get in trouble, and are allowed to treat everyone else like trash.
- The sports players and really smart kids get away with everything and the normal kids get detentions and suspensions just for being late and uniform violations. . . .

Schools' lack of action when bullying and harassment are reported:

- They never punish the people who are harassing students. It's like we get punished more.
- Some [kids] teased me for days, months. I tell the teacher, they say they'll see what they can do about it and nothing happens. I tell my parents, they talk to them, and they still don't do anything helpful. They stopped teasing me when I punched them.
- If a kid is getting picked on, they turn to a teacher who says, "I'll take care of it" and never does,—then [the kid] gets picked on more for telling, so that's when you take control and put matters into your own hands and deal with it your way. That's how people become violent.

As shown in the final set of quotations, victimization was a frequently cited rationale for becoming violent. Over and over, students described peer behaviors of teasing, taunting, and bullying that led to their feeling angry enough to hit. Although the group categorized as "violent" was more likely to admit being angry enough to hit than the group categorized as "nonviolent," it is notable that 75% of all youth surveyed in this study admitted being angry enough to hit someone.

Schools Need to Assist Students Who Feel Alienated

The loneliness and alienation of violent youth from their classmates, so clearly evident in this study, bring to mind the words Columbine shooter Eric Harris wrote in his journal: "I hate you people for leaving me out of so many fun things. You people had my phone number, and I asked and all, but no no no no no, don't let the weird-looking Eric kid come along." Although a host of school violence-prevention programs promote conflict resolution and problem-solving skills, perhaps there is insufficient attention to the alienation of disliked and lonely students. Findings of the study suggest that interventions are needed to increase the social competence and connectedness of alienated students. . . .

Early identification of youth at risk for, or involved in, violence must become a national priority.

[S]tudents expressed frustration regarding school officials' inaction when they reported substantive problems of harassment and bullying.

Female students . . . reported that school officials failed to take their complaints about bullying seriously. Relational aggression was often downplayed, and sometimes the victim herself was blamed. Students at Columbine High likewise said their teachers and staff did not seem to notice the bullying and aggression that had become part of the school culture. Fear of bullying causes more than 160,000 children to skip school every day. . . .

Reducing victimization, then, is one way to begin reducing youth violence. Many schools are implementing the Olweus Bullying Prevention Program, which is based on extensive research. . . . In a Los Angeles school, students (and their parents) sign contracts stipulating that no child can be teased or ridiculed on the basis of his/her appearance, gender, family, or grades. The Ophelia Project focuses on the relational type of aggression that is more frequently employed by girls. The project includes a schoolwide training program, guidelines for parents, and use of high-school mentors to teach younger girls how to deal with relational aggression.

Anger-management programs can help reduce students' tendencies to solve problems with physical or relational aggression. Such programs focus on arousal management (calming down with relaxation or meditation techniques) and constructive anger expression (using words, not fists, to settle disputes). As shown in this study, discussion of anger is inversely correlated with feeling angry enough to hit someone. . . . Anger discussion was positively correlated with being liked by classmates, suggesting that students who feel more secure in their interpersonal relationships may feel more secure in disclosing negative emotions. Greater use of anger discussion was associated with decreased suppression or somatization of anger and decreased loneliness.

Cognitive behavioral therapy has proved to be effective with a wide variety of angry clients, including aggressive children and juvenile delinquents. Most successful school programs, such as the Peaceful Conflict Resolution and Violence Prevention Curriculum and the Responding in Peaceful and Positive Ways Program, are based on cognitive-behavioral concepts. Tailoring such programs to specific subgroups, based on gender and/or race, may be beneficial, although more research is necessary.

A . . . limitation of the study is its cross-sectional design, prohibiting discovery of answers to chicken-and-egg questions such as: Does violent behavior precede or follow disconnectedness from peers and school? Does perception of unfair school discipline precede or follow dislike of school and penalties for angry acting-out? Few studies have traced the trajectory of violent youth over time, illuminating crucial turning points.

A broader focus includes not only the child, but also his or her peers, teachers, and school administrators.

One retrospective study, involving youths (ages 15–18) already incarcerated for murder, provides some clues regarding the trajectory. In each boy's life, there was a critical traumatic event that set him on the pathway to violent crime. The event in some cases was being bullied or assaulted, in other cases not being able to protect a mother being assaulted, being placed in foster care or special education, or witnessing a shooting. These events occurred when the boys were aged between 9 and 14. Common to all events were reactions of shame and fear, compounded by the boy's inability to talk with anyone about these feelings. All of the boys began getting in trouble in school (fighting, getting suspended) and eventually lost their connection to school, dropping out around age 13. . . . The boys felt that no one wanted them in the school anyway. Future research must examine such critical events more closely, with an eye toward swift and effective preventive and remedial interventions that can be undertaken by schools, juvenile justice officials, and mental healthcare providers.

Schools Need to Implement Prevention Measures

Mental health nurses should advocate for adoption of the national agenda developed by the Commission for the Prevention of Youth Violence (2000). Included in the Commission's report were several recommendations that have particular relevance to this study: instituting a comprehensive, evidence-based violence-prevention curriculum in every school (K–12); implementing alternative school programs to provide a safety net for students who have been expelled; and expanding screening and support services within schools to ensure that youth at risk for violence are identified and have access to appropriate monitoring and treatment. Early identification of youth at risk for, or involved in, violence must become a national priority. . . .

With regard to fostering climate change in schools, mental health nurses could be involved in provision of both direct and indirect interventions, including consultations with teachers, school nurses, and other staff, family-centered services, and preventive strategies to promote children's mental health. Our study clearly shows how important it is to consider the school environment as a determinant of violent behavior. In the past, professionals have focused almost exclusively on the pathology of individual children in accordance with the medical model. A broader focus includes not only the child, but also his or her peers, teachers, and school administrators. Students who are being bullied need to feel that the staff is going to take definitive action on their behalf. Staff must be made aware that the popular technique of peer mediation may be ineffective in situations of bullying because there is a power imbalance between the bully and the victim. . . .

It is time for Americans to pay greater attention to healthy school environments.

In order to take proper action, the power dynamics of the school must be understood. Mental health nurses could assist school nurses and teachers to conduct an assessment of the power dynamics of the school. Such an assessment could be an important step toward creation of a better climate. . . .

It is time for Americans to pay greater attention to healthy school environments. We concur with the assertion . . . that "school settings can either lessen or compound risk factors (e.g., parent relationships, poverty, neighborhood effects) that children bring to the classroom." Every child should have an opportunity to learn, and to interact with classmates and teachers, in a safe environment that facilitates emotional intelligence and psychological well-being.

Schools' Aggressive Strategies Result in Declining Rates of School Violence

Amanda Paulson

Amanda Paulson is a staff writer for the Christian Science Monitor.

In this small town just outside Chicago, several hundred restless Garfield Elementary students were summoned to the school auditorium last week for a lecture on gang violence. The assembly—spurred in part by Maywood's recent spate of homicides—is part of a wider effort, both in the district and nationwide, to combat violence at younger and younger ages.

Ever since Columbine, schools have been far more vigilant in responding, almost instantly, to violence. But it's their turn toward proactive, preventive approaches that may be paying off: A federal report released . . . [in December 2004] shows that non-fatal violence dropped dramatically between 1992 and 2002. While some data show an uptick since then, and a rise in school-related violent deaths for 2003–04, many laud schools' aggressive intervention on everything from bullying to bombs.

Prevention Programs Are Effective

In Massachusetts, for instance, officials at Marshfield High School were able to discover and avert what appeared to be a Columbine-style style plot on the part of two students to attack their school . . . [in the fall of 2004].

Amanda Paulson, "Why School Violence is Declining," *Christian Science Monitor*, December 6, 2004. www.csmonitor.com. Copyright © 2004 The Christian Science Publishing Society. All rights reserved. Reproduced by permission from *Christian Science Monitor* (www.csmonitor.com).

And in Boston, Fairbanks, Alaska, and Los Angeles, a nonprofit called Peace Games runs classes that combine civics, community service, and lessons on combatting hate-filled dialogue.

The district is trying to reach students at younger and younger ages, starting programs on character development and anger management back in elementary school.

Maywood, for its part, has seen 20 homicides . . . [in 2004], and gangs are widespread in the town of 27,000. This fall [2004], a young man was shot and killed in the parking lot of the local Proviso East High School while waiting to pick his brother up from school. Two other Proviso East students were killed in the past school year, and one student was stopped from bringing a loaded gun to school. As a result, the district is trying to reach students at younger and younger ages, starting programs on character development and anger management back in elementary school. "Here, violence is just petty things, like play fighting and name calling, but that's where it starts," says assistant principal Gwendolyn Wade after a school assembly held to address gang issues.

Administrators around the country seem to agree—and not just in crime-infested areas. The 1999 Columbine massacre [in Colorado], and the spate of school shootings from Springfield, Ore., to Jonesboro, Ark., served as a wakeup call to many districts. Schools installed metal detectors and honed crisis response plans, but many have also increased preventive work, targeting bullying and drawing the community into the conversation.

Variety of Prevention Strategies Is Key to Success

Experts increasingly agree that those "soft" approaches are key to reducing violence, and focus on violence may be one reason for the drop in school-related crime: Between 1992 and 2002, violent crime in schools fell 50 percent, from 48 victimizations per 1,000 students in 1992 to 24 per 1,000 in 2002, according to the joint report from the Bureau of Justice Statistics and the National Center for Education Statistics. It's a striking decline—one that mirrors a national drop in crime overall. . . .

One of the big things is an emphasis on bullying prevention.

But the survey itself isn't all good news: Even though crime in schools dropped between 1992 and 2002, it's still dangerous for many kids outside school.

Still, there has been progress. "Schools have put a much larger focus on safety," says William Lassiter of the Center for the Prevention of School Violence at the North Carolina Department of Juvenile Justice. "One of the big things is an emphasis on bullying prevention."

He says there's no one-size-fits-all approach, and that as much as possible, he tries to involve the students in solutions. In Baltimore, where fires have been lit in trash cans, followed by school evacuations and then drive-by shootings into the crowd, "We . . . asked why they're doing this," he says. "We found out they had a new principal who wasn't enforcing discipline, and some students were scared to be in classes with other students. In this case, the root cause was the fear of the students. There were racial and ethnic tensions at one school. So we go back to see what kind of programs . . . we can put into place."

Students Are Part of the Solution

In Maywood, too, Garfield principal Stefan Fisher sees progress. The school focuses on a different trait each week—respect, responsibility, creativity. And the district has a program of "positive behavior interaction," working with students from an early age on things like negativity and aggression. Within the school walls, students are safe, says Mr. Fisher, but he worries about dangers beyond.

"The biggest challenges are the obstacles they face that their parents are feeding them [and] what they see on the streets," he says.

Kianna Washington, a bubbly eighth-grader and aspiring beautician, says she worries about the violence she might encounter at Proviso East next year, but that the school programs have helped, her to deal with incendiary encounters. "Sometimes people try to start stuff, but I just leave it alone."

. . .

Money is also in shorter supply, and . . . No Child Left Behind demands have diverted attention from safety.

A few activists, meanwhile, say that many of the campaigns are nice, but consist largely of ineffective posters and rallies. "Schools can be hostile places," says Eric Dawson, president of Peace Games. "Part of the conversation needs to be not just what do we want less of, but what do we want more of. What do we want to create?"

Mr. Dawson hopes the Peace Games classes, with their goals of service and fighting hate, will not only give kids pride in what they can do, but change adults' often negative stereotypes about teens.

"We're trying to get the country to see young people as being part of [the] solution, not just the problem," he says. "One of the great problems I see is we don't do enough prevention work. We tend to intervene when there's a crisis or do stuff when they're in 8th grade. You have to start . . . when kids are young."

Media Hype Perpetuates False Perceptions of School Violence

Mike Males

Mike Males is an author and a sociology professor at the University of California at Santa Cruz.

Monitoring the Future, an annual survey of 12,500 high school seniors by the University of Michigan's Institute for Social Research, is one of America's most widely quoted surveys on youth behavior. Its release every December provokes a media and official frenzy over student drug use. Curiously, one of the survey's most interesting findings relevant to one of this era's biggest fears is never quoted: its findings regarding school violence trends.

Despite their worshipful citation in press and official forums, self-reporting surveys are weak, highly suspect research tools. However, *Monitoring* is the only long term consistently-administered survey of school violence available, and its trends follow the crime cycles in larger society. Its finding that both white and black students report less weapons-related victimization in school today than in the 1970s is consistent with other self-reported violence (students also report fewer instances of being deliberately injured by persons without weapons, being threatened with weapons, or being threatened with any kind of violence at school). The stable, generally declining pattern of violence among white students and the higher, cyclical pattern among black students is consistent with FBI [Federal Bureau of Investigation] crime reports. . . .

Public Perceptions of School Violence

The *Monitoring* findings also directly contradict anecdotal quotes in the press from school personnel, experts, and teen-

Mike Males, "Chapter Three: The 'School Violence' and 'Kids and Guns' Hoaxes," *Kids and Guns: How Politicians, Experts, and the Press Fabricate Fear of Youth*, September 2004. http//home.earthlink.net/~mmales/contents.htm. Copyright © 2000 online book. Reproduced by permission.

book authors that today's students are far more violent than those of past generations. These anecdotal quotes also appear at odds with what most teachers report. A 1997 *Los Angeles Times* survey of 545 students, 1,100 teachers, and 2,600 parents and other adults found that 91% of students and 92% of teachers in Los Angeles (supposedly America's arch-drug/gang/gunplay capital) rated their schools as "safe." Only 14% of students had ever been in a fight at school, and only 1% had been in a fight involving a weapon.

However, adults not involved with public schools as teachers or parents—that is, ones whose impressions derive from media images and quotable authorities—were *six to 10 times more likely to rate schools as imperiled by gangs, violence, and drugs* than were the teachers and students inhabiting those schools. *Times* editors (the same ones who editorially lament lack of public support for school funding) apparently thought the public was insufficiently terrified of public schools, as its stepped-up alarmism over "school violence". . . indicates.

The politician-media-institution campaign on "youth violence" is bigoted and devoid of genuine concern for youths.

That there is some violence in public schools—led by the school shootings of 1997–2001 that received gargantuan media attention—properly draws concern, outrage, even (in cases such as the Columbine High School slaughter) horror. But there is no excuse for Americans being *surprised* that schools are not violence-free. The lack of perspective was pointed out by Justice Policy Institute president Vincent Schiraldi in a November 22, 1999, commentary in the *Los Angeles Times*:

> Nowadays, it is impossible to talk about juvenile crime and not discuss school shootings. Yet school shootings are extremely rare and not on the increase. In a population of about 50 million schoolchildren, there were approximately

55 school-associated violent deaths in the 1992–93 school year and fewer than half that in the 1998–99 school year. By comparison, in 1997, 88 people were killed by lightning—what might be considered the gold standard for idiosyncratic events. Children who are killed in the United States are almost never killed inside a school. Yes, 12 kids were killed at Columbine. But by comparison, every two days in the U.S., 11 children die at the hands of their parents or guardians.

Gunning for Students

The term "youth violence," a media and official staple, is inherently prejudicial. To understand this, consider how we treat other demographic groups. Example: About one million Orthodox Jews live in the United States. Crime statistics aren't kept by creed, but assume a half-dozen commit murder every year.

This would give Orthodox Jews one of the lowest homicide rates of any group—probably the case. That means that every two months, on average, an Orthodox Jew is arrested for murder. Let's further assume that powerful political demagogues want to depict Jews as the font of violence, and the major media and institutions, as always, go along. Every couple of months, then, the press erupts, headlining "another Jew violence" tragedy, with sensational pictures and overwrought speculation as to "why Jews are so violent." The press and politicians resolutely ignore thousands of intervening murders by non-Jews, including murders of Jews by Gentiles, while connecting every Jewish homicide, no matter how occasional, into a "spate of Jew killings." Conservatives angrily demand tougher policing of Jews. Liberals blame violent Jewish cultural messages. Politicians and private institutions form a National Campaign to Prevent Jew Violence.

We need not add the *sieg-heils* [Nazi chant] to realize that equating Jews and violence isn't an expression of science or genuine concern, but rank anti-Semitism. Linking an entire population class with a negative behavior practiced by only a few of its members is bigotry, regardless of which group is singled out. The politician-media-institution campaign on "youth violence" is bigoted and devoid of genuine concern for youths. Real concern would involve lamenting the major causes of violence against youths, yet politicians and institutions deploring "school violence" and pushing the National Campaign to Prevent Youth Violence concern themselves only with the tiny fraction of murdered children and youth that is politically advantageous to highlight while downplaying larger dangers to the young. . . .

In his December 20, 1999, *Time* magazine commentary on the Columbine massacre, Cornell University human development professor and *Lost Boys* author James Garbarino makes a startling point. Ninety percent of teenage killers he's familiar with "conform to a pattern in which the line from bad parenting and bad environments to murder is usually clear . . . abuse, neglect and emotional deprivation at home . . . racism, poverty, the drug and gang cultures."

But the issue is not quantity, but quality. *Time* and the country wanted to fixate on the 10% who, at least within the limits of psychologists' understanding (severe limits indeed, one might argue), constitute the youthful murderers Garbarino claims "have loving parents and are not poor"—that is, who display neither of the two basic prerequisites for mayhem. These are the "KIDS Without a Conscience" gracing the cover of *People*. . . .

The Media Portrays All Teens, But Not Adults, as Potential Killers

Are youthful killers being treated unfairly, then? No—youthful *killers* are not being mistreated, except in the sense that their evil deeds are more likely to be featured in the press and deplored by luminaries than similar murders by adults. . . . The unfairness involves the fact that middle-aged killers are treated by the press and experts as crazed individuals committing isolated acts while youthful killers are treated as part of a connected pattern demonstrating today's younger generation is uniquely barbaric. . . .

Adult gun tragedy and youth gun tragedy are just two names for the same problem.

The "post-Columbine" events proved the school shootings were not a youth, but a "dissed suburban male" phenomenon. The crucial point being missed is that [Dylan] Klebold, [Eric] Harris, [Kip] Kinkel, and other middle-class student gunmen had practically nothing in common with other *kids* (their isolation, in fact, was a big part of their rage), but they had a lot in common with *adult* middle-class mass killers. . . .

[In a 2000 *New York Times* analysis of rampage killings since 1950] there was "an extremely high association between violence and mental illness." Half had been formally diagnosed with serious maladies, led by schizophrenia and depression. When it came to ignoring warning signs of catastrophe, psychiatrists, family members, and peers were equally blind. Rampage killers overwhelmingly were male (96 of 102) and white (79). . . .

Adults Are the Common Perpetrators, Not Juveniles

Children and Guns [on October 1999 Children's Defense Fund's (CDF) report] is particularly disturbing because it so casually omits the crucial contexts of gun violence by youths and instead employs statistical duplicity to advance schemes its own data show are woefully ineffective. The report notes that 37,000 "children" under age 20 (again, 18- and 19-year-olds are designated "children" or "adults," as convenient) died from gunfire from 1990 through 1997. This tragedy was compounded by the CDF's failure to point out forcefully that youth shootings are inevitable in a nation in which 250,000 adults 20 and older died from guns during the same period—or that American adults shoot many times more kids than adults shoot in all other Western nations put together. "Children" and "adults" may be separable in Washington-lobby theory, but in real life, their fates are tightly intertwined.

My calculations using the same National Center for Health Statistics data the CDF cites show the state-by-state correlation between the rate of gun death among children and among adults for the 1990s is a staggering 0.88 (on a maximum scale of 1.00). In simple terms, in states where lots of adults kill or die from guns, lots of kids kill or die from guns; in states where adults are safer, kids are safer. This near one-to-one correlation indicates that *focusing on "kids and guns" is useless; adult gun tragedy and youth gun tragedy are just two names for the same problem.*

Five times more juvenile victims were killed by adults than were killed by other juveniles.

The correlation between adult gun-death rates and youth gun-death rates is one of the highest I've seen in behavior science. It is thousands of times more significant than the widely touted, but weak correlations between youths' patronage of violent media and real-life violence, which typically average around 0.10. It means that those who are concerned about America's gun carnage should stop diverting attention with side issues like media and video game violence, or politically-safe fantasies that we can allow adults to have guns but somehow keep them away from teenagers, and get to the real issue: American adults handle guns with monumental carelessness and malintent, and "kids and guns" is just the junior version of "adults and guns."

In that regard, the CDF makes two revolutionary admissions: "children are more likely to be killed by adults than (by) other children" and "schools are one of the safest places for our children. Children are far more likely to be killed after school, in their own homes, or in their friends' homes than in school." These insights should push the debate toward focusing on guns, not the age of the shooter. But, in spite of this—or perhaps *because* they point to revolutionary shakeup—these vital truths are ignored in the remainder of CDF's report, as in the gun squabble generally.

The number-one fact neither side in the gun debate wants to talk about: adults shoot kids. The FBI's tabulation of 6,240 homicides in 2001 for which the age of killer and victim are known repeated the typical pattern: just 113 (2%) involved a juvenile under age 18 killing another juvenile. However, 610 (10%) involved an adult killing a juvenile. Thus, *five times more juvenile victims were killed by adults than were killed by other juveniles.* Nor do juveniles reciprocate by killing adults—252 homicides (4% of the total) involved a person under 18 killing a person 18 or older. The remaining 5,265 murders (84%) involved adults killing adults. . . .

Adults murder more kids every three days than student killers do in a year.

However, these crucial, distressing points were buried in the CDF's sensational press statements and poster campaign—the images most people will see. Its posters, depicting Columbine High's shooting aftermath and steely-eyed youths aiming handguns, screamed, "Remember when the only thing kids were afraid of at school was a pop quiz?" What clichéd cowardice.

Clearly, the CDF isn't up to confronting the adult violence FBI and Department of Justice figures show kills 95% of murdered children and 70% of murdered teens. Four of the five sidebar anecdotes in the CDF report depict children shooting children. The report lists the school shootings as "simply the latest wake-up calls for what has been happening every day in America for a very long time." It is troubling that the same child advocates who ringingly deplore "children killing children," "youth violence," and "guns in school" gingerly tiptoe around the fact that adults murder more kids every three days than student killers do in year. . . .

Poverty Is a Strong Indicator for Violence

As will be shown, the true villain is not race or age. Both within and between racial and ethnic groups, poverty is strongly connected to gun demise (the correlation between child poverty rates and child gun death rates by state is 0.58, also very high). The CDF, one of the few groups to raise the issue of child poverty in the 1990s, seems to soft-pedal that issue today. It fails to point out that reducing poverty is the single biggest step toward reducing gun violence both by adults and youths. . . .

In November 1999, I prepared a report for the California Attorney General's Juvenile Gun Violence Prevention Advisory Committee on the trends, levels, and factors in "youth gun violence." Contrary to expectations, I found that even in a state with an enormous gun toll (43,000 killed from 1990 through 1999), the vast majority of adolescents are not in substantial danger of death by firearms, nor are they in more danger than adolescents of past decades. California's "kids and guns" problem is highly concentrated and appears to result from "non-youth" forces, not from teenage behaviors. . . .

As poverty rates increase nine-fold . . . murder rates jump 700%, gun death rates triple, and gun homicides leap nine-fold.

In recent decades, teenage gun fatalities have remained low and have declined or remained constant among the following population groups in [California]: younger teens ages 10–14, female teens, white (non-Latino) teens, teens in wealthier counties such as Ventura and San Mateo, and deaths by accident, suicide, and undetermined intent. For these groups, gun death rates are minimal and, where homicide is the primary cause, tend to be shot by persons outside their group. From 1985 to 2000, gun death rates among white teens declined by 48% for boys and by 72% for girls.

As poverty rates increase nine-fold from the richest white youths to the poorest youths of color, murder rates jump 700%, gun death rates triple, and gun homicides leap nine-fold. Middle-income white and nonwhite youth are in between. While the public and policy makers are understandably horrified by school shootings, it appears that in California (and, most likely, the nation as a whole), both murder arrest and firearms mortality rates among white (non-Latino) teenagers plummeted to their lowest levels in two to three decades in 1997, and fell further through 2001. . . .

The most salient cause of what we call "youth gun violence" is "adult gun violence," and its antecedent in poverty. In California's 16 most populous counties (populations exceeding 500,000) during the 1990s, rates of teenage gun fatality vary by 650% (from 3 per 100,000 youths in Ventura County to 22 in neighboring Los Angeles). Variations within races are equally dramatic. For example, white teens in San Bernardino are four times more likely to die by guns than white teens in Ventura, and Asian youths in Sacramento are seven times more at risk than Asian youths in Santa Clara (San Jose). The wide variations in teenage gun death rates closely track variations in rates of adult gun death. In turn, rates of child, youth, and adult gun casualty are closely related to poverty, which is not surprising since poverty is a strong predictor of homicide. The correlation between teenage gun fatality and youth poverty rates for California's major counties in 1995–99 is 0.75; for all childhood gun deaths and injuries and youth poverty rates, even higher (0.82). . . .

Violence Prevention Programs Should Include Everyone, Not Just Teens

The complex patterns of gun death in California suggest caution about popular solutions. Major efforts to "get guns out of the hands of kids" are problematic in a state where some 30 million guns are privately owned, as well as inefficient given that the large majority of youth who have access to guns are not at risk from them. Efforts to reduce or prevent gun acquisition by persons of all ages who are unsuited to have them (surveys showing widespread, careless gun storage and handling by adults suggest that *most* people are unsuited) through laws and strict training requirements are also beneficial. An age-integrated "California firearms violence and prevention campaign" would be preferable to one which focuses only on "juveniles." Other than in the artificial world of political convenience, there seems to be no material difference between youths and the adults around them when it comes to firearms tragedy.

Most Campus Crimes Can Be Prevented

Nancy Fitzgerald

Nancy Fitzgerald is the contributing editor at Careers and Colleges, *a college and university guide.*

It was the tail end of finals week, and Erica Madden, a sophomore at Indiana University in Bloomington, had gone to bed early while her roommates celebrated the finish of another school year. When the party was over at about 3 in the morning, the roommates left to drive their friends back home, leaving Madden in the apartment alone—or so they thought.

As soon as they pulled off in their cars, a couple of uninvited guests sashayed in through the apartment's unlocked door and proceeded to help themselves to what they wanted. When Madden's roommates returned, their four stereo speakers were gone, and there was an empty space where their prized recliner used to be. "It was kind of creepy," Madden admits, "to think that they were in the apartment while I was sleeping. In theory, it was our fault since we left the door open. But we left it open most of the time—we never felt threatened."

Campus security directors around the country agree: She should have been more cautious. "Once students get that familiar feeling on campus," says Dolores Stafford, director of police at George Washington University in Washington, D.C., "they end up feeling like it's home in a different way than they should. They feel like it's their mom's house." And that kind of complacency can lead to unhappy experiences like Madden's.

Nancy Fitzgerald, "Special Report: Safety on Campus: Most Schools Are Safe Havens for Learning. But Dangers—Crime, Alcohol Abuse, Fire Hazards—Do Exist. Knowing the Realities Can Help You Protect Yourself." *Careers and Colleges*, March–April, 2004. Copyright © 2004 Alloy Education. All rights reserved. Reproduced by permission.

Abstaining from Alcohol Increases Student Safety

The good news for incoming college students is that campus crime has actually been declining. According to the Department of Education, burglaries at colleges have dropped by half from 2000 to 2002. Increased awareness has certainly helped students to protect themselves. You should begin by knowing the safety records at your college choices. You probably won't find a crime report in a college viewbook, but thanks to a law passed by Congress in 1990, that information is easy to get. The law requires all colleges to post their crime statistics at http://ope.ed.gov/security [the U.S. Department of Education's Office of Postsecondary Education website].

Krueger's tragic death illustrates a critical lesson for every student heading off to college: The biggest danger you may face there will be alcohol.

Crime is just one of the threats on campuses—students also have to cope with the dangers of alcohol, drugs, and fire. . . .

Scott Krueger was really smart. He had the brains and drive to make it into the Massachusetts Institute of Technology, one of the nation's top schools, where he planned to major in computer science. But just one week into his freshman year after an "Animal Night" fraternity party that featured chugging a bottle of spiced rum, he died of alcohol poisoning.

Krueger's tragic death illustrates a critical lesson for every student heading off to college: The biggest danger you may face there will be alcohol. Nationwide, 44 percent of students have engaged in binge drinking, according to the Harvard School of Public Health.

According to The Chronicle [of Higher Education] website, arrests for alcohol violations increased 4 percent from 1999 to 2001; arrests for drug violations grew by 10.2 percent.

And security officials say that not only does heavy drinking put you at risk for alcohol poisoning, it also makes you more likely to commit—or become a victim of other crimes, too. "Alcohol is behind 90 percent of campus crime," says Howard Clery, the treasurer for Security on Campus, a crime information network in King of Prussia, Pennsylvania. It's often the fuel that fires crimes such as theft, vandalism, and rape. . . .

Females Who Exercise Extreme Caution Are Safer

Kate Murray was upset about her boyfriend, who attended college in another state. So she was glad to be spending the afternoon with her friend Jim at Hofstra University in Hempstead, New York. When the freshman visited Jim's dorm room one day, she began crying.

Rarely do we find a door's been broken in—theft is usually a crime of opportunity.

"It was a vulnerable moment for me," Murray recalls. "He started to comfort me, but before I knew it, he was pinning me down. And he had turned the stereo up so loud that nobody could hear when I started screaming."

Murray had become a victim of date—or acquaintance—rape, a crime that has increased on many campuses. Safe Campuses Now reports that one in eight women will be raped during their college years, and 84 percent of them will know their assailants. Murray didn't report her incident because she was too embarrassed to talk about it.

Although most of the time date rape occurs while students are using alcohol or other drugs, that wasn't the case for Murray. "There was no alcohol involved," she says. "But people will take advantage of you if they want to." . . .

Thefts Can Be Prevented

When Seth Voeltner packed up his stuff to head for the University of Wisconsin at Stevens Point, one of the first things to go into the minivan was his dark gray Raleigh M-40 road bike. He'd worked all summer to save up the $300 to buy it, and he looked forward to using it to get around campus. But by the end of his first semester, the bike was gone.

"I never got around to buying a U-lock," he says, "I thought, 'Hey, everybody respects everybody else on this campus.' Then one day I went to the bike rack, and it was gone. It definitely made me a little less trusting."

"The biggest problem on college campuses is theft," says Ernie Leffler, director of campus police at Bentley College in Waltham, Massachusetts. "People get ripped off in academic buildings and residence halls. Students will leave their door unlocked and run down to the cafeteria, and come back to find their laptop stolen. Rarely do we find a door's been broken broken in—theft is usually a crime of opportunity." . . .

Students Get Expelled for Dangerous Pranks

In January 2000, a [fire] . . . swept through a dorm at Seton Hall University in South Orange, New Jersey, killing three students and injuring more than 50 others. After repeated false alarms, students simply didn't take the real thing seriously enough. Over the past six years, Seton Hall has expelled three students for pulling false alarms.

"Fire safety is a huge concern," says Dan Werner, director of security and safety at Kenyon College in Ohio. "When you don't take it seriously, you're putting hundreds of lives at risk."

Paying attention to the fire codes in your dorm, he insists, is critical—whether or not the building is outfitted with sprinklers. "Especially for first-year students," he says, "peer pressure is just about as powerful as gravity. But if somebody is using a hot plate against the regulations, you've got to stand up and say, 'It's my life you're putting in jeopardy.'"

A recent national survey of college campuses reported that 67 percent of colleges have at least one dorm without a sprinkler system. And the false alarm is just as deadly elsewhere as it was at Seton Hall: 37 percent of schools surveyed reported that false alarms are a problem on their campuses. "We don't even call them false alarms anymore," says Werner. "They're malicious alarms." . . .

Chapter 2

What Factors Contribute to School Violence?

Chapter Preface

Years ago, no one would imagine that crime and violence at the public school level would mean rape, robbery, murder, arson, and many other heinous crimes. According to researchers, urban environments tend to have higher poverty rates. This concentrated poverty lends itself to more violent crimes and a higher incidence of drug and alcohol abuse. The School Violence Resource Center suggests that an urban environment has certain "risk factor domains." These domains include individual risk factors, family risk factors, community risk factors, and school risk factors. Individual risk factors include delinquent friends, aggressiveness of the individual, any substance abuse, lower intelligence, and birth complications. Family risk factors include any history of family crime and violence, lower or lack of expectations by parents, lack of parental monitoring, parental involvement in drugs, and child abuse and neglect. Community factors include the availability of weapons, drugs, violence, large numbers of broken homes, high transient populations, and economic deprivation within the immediate area. School risk factors include such things as early delinquent behavior, academic failure, lack of commitment to school, and gang involvement.

Samuel L. Blumenfeld, M.D., author of several books on education, has a more simplified explanation for today's school violence: psychotropic drugs. Millions of school children are now diagnosed with attention deficit/hyperactivity disorder (ADHD) and are prescribed Ritalin, one of the most powerful drugs given to children. Many of the school shooters over recent years were taking medications: Eric Harris, eighteen, one of the Columbine shooters, was taking the antidepressant Luvox. T.J. Solomon, fifteen, who shot and wounded six classmates at Heritage High School in Conyers, Georgia, was on Ritalin for depression. Shawn Cooper, fifteen, who fired two shotgun rounds, narrowly missing students and teachers at his high school in Notus, Idaho, was also on Ritalin for bipolar disorder. Kip Kinkel, fifteen, was on Ritalin and Prozac. He murdered his parents and then went on to school where he fired on students in the cafeteria, killing two and wounding twenty two.

Edward M. Hallowell, M.D., and John J. Ratey, M.D., authors of *Driven to Distraction*, write, "ADD [attention deficit disorder] lives in the biology of the brain and the central nervous system. The exact mechanism underlying ADD remains unknown." In Dr. Blumenfeld's words, "We are dealing with a neurological enigma wrapped in a biological mystery." He questions if it is possible "that there is a much simpler explanation for ADD," and suggests that "the school atmosphere itself is causing the extreme distractibility and impulsive behavior that are the major symptoms of ADD." When Dr. Blumenfeld was in school, he noted that the desks and seats were bolted to the floor and could not be moved. The walls were generally bare. The room was clean and orderly. The room was also silent. The teacher was the focus of attention. Thus, there was no ADD. Impulsive behavior would have resulted in discipline from the principal. But now, he observes, kids are seated around tables, pestering one another, chatting and interrupting. Each child is doing something different, such as writing, reading, or drawing. One child may be under a table reading a book; another may be sprawled on the floor drawing a large picture. The walls, too, provide a source of distraction. Dr. Blumenfeld notes that the walls are "covered with every conceivable kind of distraction: dinosaurs, Mickey Mouse, bulletin boards, pictures of animals, travel posters, you name it. Then there are fish tanks, gerbils, and rabbits to grab one's attention. Mobiles hang from the ceiling, swaying in the breeze. Anything and everything that could possibly distract a child is there." He asks if it is "any wonder that so many children suffer the equivalent of a cognitive breakdown in American schools? The entire school configuration is designed to cause distraction, inattention, frustration, impulsiveness, hatred, anger, and violence. And the only way that many children can be forced to endure that atmosphere is by drugging them."

Whether the forces that drive kids to violence are biological, pharmacological, or environmental, the authors in the following chapter debate the causes and contributing factors to school violence.

School Shooters View the World as Unjust

Tom O'Connor

Tom O'Connor is a professor at North Carolina Wesleyan College.

If every mention of suicide is a cry for help, then every instance of school shooting must be a scream of rage. Nationwide, since 1992, it seems (and in some places before then), students began violating every sanctity or taboo that existed In school decorum. It's not just high schools and colleges, but the middle schools and elementary schools, as well, where violence is spreading. Campus crime is a special case that is discussed later. Yale professor Jerome Singer has tracked numerous problem behaviors in kindergarten through fourth grade, and surmises that some problem children have just never grown out of their "terrible twos." Ask any teacher who has been teaching for some time, and they'll tell you classroom discipline is a lot harder these days. Some say our school systems are out of control, and some media pundits refer to schools as "killing fields" where students, teachers, administrators, and staff aren't safe anymore. A study by the CDC [Centers for Disease Control and Prevention] in 1995 found that nearly one-fourth of students regularly carry a weapon to school, and even though student assaults on other students are the most common type of school violence, other studies have consistently found that, in any given year, 28% of teachers are verbally abused, 15% are threatened with injury, and 3% are physically attacked by a student. In this lecture, some probable hypotheses for the phenomenon of school violence are examined, with a focus upon the psyche and mindset of school shooters and adolescents today. . . .

Tom O'Connor, "School Violence: Why Johnny Shoots," November 30, 2005. http://faculty.ncwc.edu. Reproduced by permission of the author.

A Commentary on the Sorry State of Today's Generations

It's easy to blame it on peers, violent music, TV, or computer games, but doesn't the real problem have something to do with the sorry state of education today? Or the way baby boomers dumped on the children of the 70's and 80's? Regarding the first possibility, it can be argued that most schools today are *under-funded, poorly staffed, overly regimented, bleak, boring places* stuck on perpetuating an 18th-century model of classroom teaching complete with bells, bad furniture, forced group activities, overpriced textbooks, the joke we call cafeterias, grade inflation, clueless self-serving administrators, and teachers who can't wait to update their resumes in hopes of getting a better job elsewhere only to be replaced by an endless stream of second-careerists and teacher-wannabes who want to take their turn at it. It can also be argued that teachers spend way too much time on building self-esteem at the expense of important content. . . .

Other possibilities exist to explain the sorry state of today's youth. . . . [Gregg] Easterbrook [writer and editor] refers to the mental condition of today's generations as "collapse anxiety" which means people have so much nowadays, it's hard to expect the coming years to bring more. Instead of being happy, we fear the economy will collapse, our natural resources will run out, or some crazy act of super-terrorism will wipe out the human race. [Researchers Robert A.] Emmons and [Michael E.] McCullough have also conducted gratitude research and found that young people today are sorely lacking in dispositions related to happiness and gratitude.

If you were born between 1965 and 1984, then you belong to the *Hip Hop Generation* (if you're black), and to *Generation X* (if you're white). . . . If you were born after those dates, then you are a *13th Gen*. . . . If you were born before those dates, then you belong to the *Superfly* generation (if black) and the *baby boomers* (if white). The defining features of the

Hip Hop Generation are anti-intellectualism, irresponsible parenthood, immense wealth, power, and glorification of criminal lifestyle. The defining features of Generation X (that are shared with the Hip Hop Generation) are bitterness, a tendency to avoid personal responsibility, a tendency to play the blame game, and a tendency to demand fairness in outcomes rather than work the process for achieving fairness in outcomes. All of these characteristics are typical, and easily predicted, of *any post-segregation population in any postmodern society that has moved beyond its Civil Rights stage of development*. Some of these characteristics explain why students seem to resist learning and why they often behave in such mystifying ways toward teachers. Even students who apply themselves to learning may be letter-perfect in a school subject and still fail spectacularly in transferring that knowledge from the classroom to the real world, and conversely, success in the real world is no guarantee of success in school. . . . Almost all the literature suggests that employers who hire recent graduates report more disciplinary incidents of unruliness and workplace violence.

Some of those who go all the way [in carrying out plans to perpetrate a school shooting] are straight-A, ideal, all-American students from stable and good families.

Turning to how previous generations have "dumped" on today's generations, consider that 22 percent of children under the age of eighteen live in poverty, not relative poverty, but *absolute poverty*. That's just one of the impacts of a +50% divorce rate. A known fact in criminology is that adolescents from lower socioeconomic status (SES) families regularly commit more violence than youth from higher SES levels. An upwardly mobile family system has always been the best way to multiply capital, and the secret of generational success has always been having a steady family who works at moving up together year after year, not some part-time serial parent who works at making ends [meet] and reinforces some get-rich-quick scheme. The latter tends to produce over-idealistic, go-it-alone dot.com millionaire fantasies with cause a strain toward crime. Families not only pass on money, but important values like love, honor, obedience, responsibility, accountability, honesty, commitment, loyalty, respect, and work ethic. When it is said that *today's generations have it tougher* than previous generations, what is primarily meant by this is that, today, there are more extreme conditions of declining social morality and family commitment to social mobility than the generations before. It also doesn't help that today's generation grew up with *nothing but sound bites instead of reasonable discourse about social problems*. . . .

The Adolescent Psyche of School Shooters

School violence is unlike workplace violence. The offender doesn't "snap" and suddenly go wild. Instead, they plan, acquire weapons, and frequently tell others what they are planning. A lot of kids in schools carry out such planning and announcing. The Secret Service, which has studied assassins extensively, says with school shootings, there's no profile or checklist of warning signs to differentiate the planners from those likely to carry out their plans. Some of those who go all the way are straight-A, ideal, all-American students from stable and good families. Some are children of divorce and loners. A few of them write poetry, songs, or drawings that show some fascination with death. Some of the things they say to their friends are: "I think it would be cool to kill people" or "I think I could get away with killing people," but again, neither the extent of planning nor the extent of announcing are reliable indicators.

School shooters don't usually suffer from any sort of mental illness, although many are described as desperate and depressed. The most common attribute is a sense of disconnectedness—from society, and from wanting to end some generalized sense of unjustness or unfairness of it all. Homicidal urges develop out of a sense of being overwhelmed with the mundane details of life, as opposed to suicidal urges which more likely arise from the stressful, extraordinary events in life. The following are some typical comments made by school shooters when interviewed after their shootings:

- "I'm not insane. I'm just angry and miserable because people like me are mistreated every day." [*Luke Woodham*]
- "I'm just full of rage. Everyone and everything, it seems, is against me." [*Kip Kinkel*]
- "My hatred for humanity forced me to do what I did." [*Eric Houston*]
- "It wasn't that I particularly disliked anybody. I just wanted to kill people." [*Scott Pennington*]

The more typical school shooter perceives some grievous injustices being done all around them.

A common theme in the school shooter's psyche is a sense that life's not worth fixing, and this is *not* the same as a sense of life's not worth living. In most cases, the shooter has not withdrawn from life, but the responsibility for exerting any effort at achieving any changes for chances for achievement in life anymore. In this sense, school shooting is similar to celebrity crime, or crimes by the wealthy and famous, for what does one do when they've reached the top? This makes sense when we consider that some of the school shooters were straight-A success stories in their schools. The most significant question to ask is *Why the school?* Why do shooters choose the school as the place to carry out their acts? The answer that one typically gets back from a school shooter is "Because that's where most of my pain and suffering was" or "That's where the people were."

Hypotheses and Models of School Violence

Violent school shooters aren't freaks or geeks with problems in anger management. Surely a few have been bullied by cliques or classmates, but the more typical school shooter perceives some grievous injustice being done all around them. Such people are typically introverted and self-conscious types. Columbine's shooters, Dylan Klebold and Eric Harris, who killed themselves after their rampage, seem to fit a had-it-with-education model. Their planning and announcement cycles were clearly aimed at the school environment as both the problem and solution for their troubles.

Frequently, 13- and 14-year [old] boys (the typical age and sex of shooters) all seem to say the same thing—"I was angry, and I killed them because they mistreated me every day." That's exactly what was said by Evan Ramsey for example, an Alaskan 1997 school shooter nicknamed "Screech," after a geeky character in the TV show, *Saved by the Bell.* The theme of being mistreated before going on a killing rampage is a theme that comes up again and again in the anecdotal evidence, and, indeed, the peer mistreatment model seems to be a popular lay explanation of school violence.

Another proximate factor is a decline in the quality of communication with parents and adults.

Other experts say the most recent spat of school shootings starting in 1997 hallmarked the contagion model set by Luke Woodham, a 16-year-old in Mississippi who killed his mother and two classmates, wounding seven others. Woodham told the police who took his confession, "I guess everyone is going to remember me now." Serving multiple life sentences, he has since expressed remorse. Nathaniel Brazill, the 13-year-old who killed his language-arts teacher in Florida said, "I guess I'm going to be all over the news now." Obviously, some sort of copycat effect or imitation is going on, consistent with contagion models.

Another proximate factor in many of the shooters' lives, a factor they have in common with perpetrators of workplace violence, is a girlfriend relationship gone bad, some kind of teen romance model. Jacob Davis used a magnum bolt-action rifle to shoot his girlfriend's ex-lover at his Tennessee high school in 1998. At the time, he also received news of a computer science scholarship to college. He bad been brooding for over three months on his girlfriend's disclosure that she slept with another boy before him. The problem with this model is that, of course, not all school shooters had romantic problems.

Another proximate factor is a decline in the quality of communication with parents and adults. Parents seem to be the more important factor here, in relation to a shooter's perception of their peers. What this means is that when peer communication declines, the youth wants to be able to talk to his parents (in compensation for a loss of communication with peers), but cannot, and therefore generalizes some sense of disconnection across settings. The transmission and consistency of aggression across settings (such as the home and school) is the person-environment model. This model integrates children's family functioning with their relationships with peers outside the home.

Psychiatrists stake their claim on the possibility that school shooters are suffering from mental illness. Prosecutors stake their argument by saying shooters are just unredeemable psychopaths. Medical professionals commonly diagnose depression with psychotic features. Other experts say shooters have schizophrenia or its precursors. Sixty percent of school shooters are taking some type of prescribed medication at the time of their shootings, something for insomnia, sleep disorder, or attention deficit disorder. It's easy to blame Ritalin for family and school problems, and genetics for motivational problems, but doesn't someone need to ask about what conditions prompted the need for medication and/or therapy?...

A Focus on College Campus Crime

With campus crime, the policy problem is different. Instead of a void or vacuum, political leaders have a tendency to throw legislation at the problem without looking into the criminology of campus crime. No less than three major pieces of legislation were passed in the 1990s:

- the Campus Crime and Security Act of 1990
- the Campus Sexual Assault Victims Bill of Rights of 1991
- the Higher Education Amendments of 1998 (the Jeanne Clery Act)

The cause of campus crime, according to most criminological expertise, is the campus culture itself. Many things that college students regard as "cool" are criminal behaviors, and college students are typically independence-oriented and more prone toward vigilantism than crime reporting. Campus crime is facilitated by an ethos of "binge drinking" and a certain mentality of sexism and racism that is widely tolerated. With rape, for example, government studies, such as those conducted by the OVC [Office for Victims of Crime], have shown that more than 50% of college females who have been raped are likely to "redefine" it as not-rape. The federal and state governments have consistently had the hardest time getting colleges to accurately report murder and manslaughter on campus as anything other than "miscellaneous incidents." Campus security is perceived as a joke on most college campuses, and legislators are reluctant to grant teachers, staff, or campus security personnel exceptions to Gun-Free Safe School

Zone provisions, as simply insisting schools be gun-free makes them so. Instead of real, practical security measures which address the causes of campus crime, most places chase after the funding sources which are readily available for fairly meaningless things like victim-related commemorative observances such as National Crime Victims' Rights Week, Domestic Violence Awareness Month, Sexual Assault Awareness Month, National Drunk and Drugged Driving Awareness Week, Mock Court Alcohol Awareness events, Rophynil and Date Rape Awareness Day, etc. The really sad thing is that government funding is plentifully available for criminologists and researchers to evaluate these futile awareness programs. This diverts scholarly attention away from real problems and solutions, and schools never quite become safer places, but the recipients of funding get to say they received a grant.

In addition, there is a serious, unrecognized mental health problem on college campuses involving a doubling of rates of depression and a tripling of rates of suicide since 1988. More college students than ever before are suffering from serious and life-threatening emotional conflicts and mental illness, and the crisis pervades campuses at every level, size, academic status, and geographic location. Mentally ill college students desperately need detection, early intervention, and ongoing treatment precisely at a time when there has been a dramatic decline in financial or administrative support for such services. The causes of college mental illness appear to be developmental issues (such as relationship, sexuality, and roommate problems) combined with academic pressures (rigor for the sake of rigor, extracurricular demands, parental expectations, and diversity issues) combined with financial problems (how to pay off college bills and plan for employment or graduate school). More and more people are getting into college who couldn't have done so before because they are on anti-depressant medication which allows them to do the minimum necessary to stay in school. Not all people with mental illness are potentially violent and dangerous, but some are, and developing adequate safeguards and protection for this admittedly low-risk threat should not be sacrificed for the cause of eliminating the stigma of mental illness.

Video Games Cause Aggressive and Violent Behavior in Youths

David Walsh, Douglas Gentile, Erin Walsh, and Nat Bennett

David Walsh is the president and founder of the National Institute on Media and the Family, established in 1996. Douglas Gentile runs the Media Research Lab at Iowa State University, where he studies media's effects on children and adults. Erin Walsh has expertise in the area of video game violence and is a training consultant for Media Wise. Nat Bennett is a writer and teacher living in New York City.

This year [2006], as always, is marked by change in the world of video games. Video game consoles that take advantage of previously unthinkable technologies have been launched by Microsoft, Nintendo and Sony. A growing body of research continues to expand our understanding of the impact electronic games have on young people. Innovation in more technologically advanced countries provides a window into the problems looming for American families. In short, the relationship between families and video games is becoming ever more complex, making an overview of the issues even more vital than before. . . .

Parental Ignorance: No Longer Bliss

As the world of video games continues to evolve, parents are falling behind. As we found last year, this year's parental survey uncovered an alarming gap between what kids say about the role of video games in their lives and what parents are willing to admit. For instance, while nearly two-thirds of surveyed parents said they had rules about how much time their

David Walsh, Douglas Gentile, Erin Walsh and Nat Bennett, "11th Annual Media Wise Video Game Report Card," November 28, 2006. www.mediafamily.org. Copyright © National Institute on Media and the Family. Reproduced by permission.

children may spend playing video games, only one third of their children said they had such rules. Perhaps parents are reluctant to confess how little they attempt to control the amount of time their kids spend in front of the screen. This much is certain: too many of us do not seem to exercise enough control. The amount of time kids spend playing video games is on the rise.

Video game addiction has led some children to fail out of school, alienate themselves from everyone in their lives and, in extreme cases, to commit suicide.

First and foremost, parents need to pay attention to the relevant research and the industry needs to stop denying research-based conclusions.

- *Who's playing?* While the industry constantly reports that the average age of the player has risen to the late twenties, a new study has found almost half of all "heavy gamers" are six- to seventeen-years-old.
- *Game time and physical health.* Our own research this year found children who spend more time playing video games are heavier, and are more likely to be classified as overweight or obese. Furthermore, playing video games in the bedroom is an added risk factor for overweight and obesity.
- *Screen time and school performance.* We found the amount of time kids spend playing video games is correlated with poorer grades in school and attention problems.
- *Violent video games and aggression.* Scientific research shows that violent video game play increases aggression in young players in the short term. Additional studies show these effects last.

Once parents realize what is at stake, based on scientific research, they should start limiting game time and keeping M-rated [mature rated, for persons seventeen and older] games away from their children. Although the Entertainment Software Rating Board (ESRB) rating system seems to underrate some games, giving Teen ratings to games that deserve Mature ratings, all agree that the M-rated games are inappropriate for kids. . . .

Video Game Addiction Hurts Kids

Video game addiction is another alarming game-related health issue. Many of the symptoms of this type of addiction are largely the same as the symptoms of other addictions including obsessive behaviors, deceitful behavior, neglecting people and responsibilities, and increased isolation. Video game addiction has led some children to fail out of school, alienate themselves from everyone in their lives, and in extreme cases, commit suicide. Some of the most popular online community games practically demand an obsessive and time-consuming approach to play. As with any addiction, once children are hooked, it is very difficult for them to quit.

South Korea has seen a recent explosion in cases of video game addiction. The South Korean government now supports more than 40 treatment programs to deal with video game and Internet addiction. If the situation in South Korea is any indication of what is to come here, we will be largely unprepared for the number and intensity of cases of such addiction. . . .

[In 2005] . . . we said that every child who plays video games is undertaking a powerful, developmental experiment—the results of which we don't understand. This is truer now than ever before. We need more research on the ways interactive entertainment affects child health and development. We must focus not only on aggression and violence, but also on health, behavior, school performance, and work skills as well as the positive effects and uses of video games. . . .

Student Survey Results

The American Academy of Pediatrics recommends no more than one to two hours of screen time per day, including time spent on video games, television, videos/DVDs, and computer use. However, our data shows that:

- Forty-two percent of children play for at least one hour per day, with 22% reporting they play for two or more. This is on top of the three hours a day the average child spends in front of the television.
- Fifteen percent of children state they feel they spend too much time playing video games. Interestingly, 26% say they play too little, suggesting what a large role games now play in young people's lives.
- One in ten (9%) admit they play so much that it sometimes hurts their homework. This finding is particularly surprising, because third-, fourth- and fifth-graders do not typically have a lot of homework.
- Over half (55%) say they sometimes try to stop playing video games so much. Children who play video games in their bedrooms play five hours more per week than children who do not play in their bedrooms.

We found that playing a large amount of violent video games increased children's risk of physical aggression in school by 42%.

Total amount of game play is not, however, the only issue that matters—the content of the games played matters greatly, too.

- We found that playing a large amount of violent video games increased children's risk of physical aggression in school by 42% over children who do not play violent video games.
- These findings held true even when the following other factors remained constant: sex, violent television exposure, parent involvement, and prior history of fights.

In short, the research demonstrates that both the *amount* and *content* of games matter. The ones who spend more time playing video games are heavier, and are more likely to be classified as overweight or obese. And confirming the results of several other studies, our survey found that the amount of time a child plays video games is correlated with receiving poorer grades in school, as reported by both parents and teachers. In addition, the amount of time spent playing video games is correlated with teacher-reported attention problems in school, also corresponding to other research which finds a link between heavy screen use and attention problems.

Parent Survey Results

The ESRB has promoted research suggesting that 74% of parents regularly use the video game ratings and 94% find them helpful in choosing games for their children. Other research, including ours, does not paint quite such a rosy picture. In our sample of 1,430 third- and fifth-grade children and their parents, we find that parents and children have very different perceptions of how involved parents are. For example, most (73%) parents say they "always" help decide what games their children may buy or rent. However, only 30% of children say their parents do. On the opposite side, only 1% of parents say they "never" help decide, in contrast to 25% of children. . . .

This pattern appears in several other places in our study. For example, when measuring the amount of time children play video games each week, parents report an average of five hours per week. When their children are asked, they report an average of nine hours per week (13 hours for boys, 6 for girls). These findings, and the gap between them, are basically identical to the national averages found in other studies. This suggests that parents may provide overly optimistic responses about their awareness of children's video game habits and their use of the ratings. . . .

Retailer Ratings Enforcement Survey Results

As in years past, we once again conducted a "sting" operation to determine if retailers are enforcing their ratings policies on M-rated games. Fourteen children between the ages of 10 and 16 (four female, 10 male) entered retail stores and attempted to purchase M-rated games without adult supervision. The sting operations took place between August and October 2006 at retail locations located in California, Illinois, Iowa, Maryland and Minnesota.

Despite years of scrutiny and repeated promises to clean up their act, it is still far too easy for kids to purchase inappropriate games.

Of the 25 sting operations, eight resulted in successful purchases (32% success rate, down from 44% in 2005, 34% in 2004, and 55% in 2003).

Eight of the purchases were attempted by girls. Girls were much less likely to be able to purchase games than boys (13% girls, 41% boys). This is a large decrease from last year (46% girls, 42% boys), but is more typical of rates we've seen in past years where girls are less able to purchase than boys (8% girls, 50% boys in 2004).

Interestingly, we see a notable split among the big retailers and stores specializing in video games. Major retailers—Best Buy, Target and Wal-Mart—emerged with perfect scores, preventing underage customers from purchasing M-rated games on every attempt. We are very encouraged to see the big retailers stepping up and keeping their promise to enforce their own policies. Unfortunately, specialty stores seem more interested in making money than anything else. Despite years of scrutiny and repeated promises to clean up their act, it is still far too easy for kids to purchase inappropriate games at such stores. . . .

Media Wise Video Game Report Card Summary and Highlights

Parental Involvement: Incomplete

Although the response of most parents to the challenge of raising kids in a world filled with video games is inadequate, it doesn't seem fair to give parents a failing grade because parents are constantly subject to mixed messages from the video game industry. While representatives of the industry encourage parents to follow the ratings which warn certain age groups away from mature content, they simultaneously deny that video games have any impact on kids. Making matters worse, the rating system itself has flaws. Parents could be, and should be, doing a lot better, but at least part of their failure can be attributed to the confusion created by the game makers.

In our survey, half of all attempts by minors to purchase M-rated games were successful at specialty stores.

Ratings Education: B

Our findings in the area of Ratings Education are nearly identical to those of last year. We are encouraged to see a visible effort by the ESRB to educate parents and retailers and a corresponding tendency on the part of retailers to educate employees and parents. Nevertheless, considering that we have found no significant progress from last year, we see room for improvement.

Retailer Policies: B

Nearly every retailer we surveyed claimed to have a policy preventing children and teens from purchasing M-rated games, an improvement from last year. Perhaps more praiseworthy, most of the employees we surveyed could articulate the policy and its importance. Clearly, public pressure in recent years has put retailers on notice.

Retailer Enforcement

Big Retailers: A

Specialty Stores: F

Although it is encouraging to find that the retailers across the board present the public with a policy to prevent the sale of M-rated games to minors, we see a remarkable gap in the performance of retailers. The big retailers such as Best Buy, Target and Wal-Mart have kept their promise to keep M-rated games out of kids' hands. In our survey, no children were sold M-rated games at these stores. Stores specializing in video games seemed to be willing to let profits take priority over enforcing the policies they claim to uphold, in our survey, half of all attempts by minors to purchase M-rated games were successful at specialty stores.

The primary finding was that adolescents who play more violent video games engage in more real-life aggressive and violent behaviors.

Console Manufacturers (Microsoft, Sony and Nintendo): A

Every new console entering the market now includes parental controls. Considering that only a few years ago such parental controls were unthinkable, this is amazing progress. The manufacturers of video game systems deserve praise for their efforts to make it easier for parents to protect their kids.

Recommendations for the Video Game Industry and Parents

1. The industry should eliminate the double messages to parents and educate them about why it is important to monitor game play and observe the ratings.
2. Specialty game stores should follow the lead of the major retailers who have fulfilled their commitment not to sell M- or Adults Only-rated games to youth.
3. There should be a universal, independent rating system.
4. More attention should be paid to the emerging problem of video game addiction.
5. Kids' bedrooms should be media-free zones.
6. Parents need to supervise their children's game playing more closely.

- Follow the ratings.
- Use Parental Controls.
- Put your kids on a media diet.
- Set limits and be willing to say "no."
- Watch what your kids watch, play what your kids play. . . .

Research on the Effects of Violent Games

Although there has been little new published research in 2006, dozens of experimental and correlational studies now document that violent video game play is related to increases in aggressive thoughts, feelings, and behaviors. . . . [In 2006, researchers] published a study in which 257 college students were randomly assigned to play one of eight violent or non-violent video games for 20 minutes. After playing the game, the students were shown a 10-minute videotape of real-life violent acts (including shootings, stabbings, prison fights, etc.) while their heart rate and galvanic skin response (both measures of arousal and stress) were measured. Students who had played one of the violent video games showed lower levels of arousal to the violent scenes. That is, 20 minutes of playing a violent video game desensitized them to images of real-life violence in the short term.

In . . . [an] experimental study, 161 nine- to 12-year-olds and 354 college students played either a violent or nonviolent video game. The primary finding was that even E-rated violent games increased children's and college students' aggressive behavior immediately after playing the game. In the correlational study, 189 high school students completed surveys about their media habits, their personalities, and their aggressive behaviors. The primary finding was that adolescents who play more violent video games engage in more real-life aggressive and violent behaviors. In the longitudinal study, 430 third-fourth- and fifth-grade students, their peers, and teachers were surveyed early and late in a school year. The primary finding was that children who played more violent video games early in the school year had changed to become more aggressive later in the school year, as reported by their peers and teachers.

Students Who Are Repeatedly Bullied Will Often Resort to Violence

John Greenya

John Greenya is a freelance writer in Washington, DC. He has written for the Washington Post, New Republic, New York Times, *and other publications.*

The nation received a shocking wake-up call about bullying when investigators revealed that the Columbine killers and other school shooters had been repeatedly bullied by classmates. On a typical school day today three out of 10 American youngsters are involved in bullying as perpetrators, victims or bystanders, and an estimated 160,000 children skip school for fear of being harassed. Bullied students are more prone to suicide, depression and poor school performance; bullies have a far higher likelihood of committing crimes as adults. At least 16 states have passed laws requiring schools to provide anti-bullying programs, but many states and school districts have been slow to act. Their reluctance may stem in part from opposition by conservative Christians, who argue that anti-bullying legislation and programs aimed at reducing sexually oriented teasing promote homosexuality and impinge on Christian students' freedom of speech. . . .

Schools Often Dismiss the Seriousness of Bullying

For many educators—and anguished parents—it took the horror of Columbine to awaken the nation to the seriousness—and pervasiveness—of bullying.

After Columbine High School students Dylan Klebold and Eric Harris massacred 12 students and a teacher and then

John Greenya, "Violence in Schools: Bullying," *CQ Researcher*, vol. 15, no. 5, February 4, 2005. Copyright © 2005 by CQ Press, published by CQ Press, a division of Congressional Quarterly Inc. All rights reserved. Reproduced by permission.

killed themselves at their school in the affluent Denver suburb of Littleton in 1999, parents told investigators that bullying had been rampant at Columbine.

Shari Schnurr, the mother of a student injured at Columbine, told the Governor's Columbine Review Commission she had discussed bullying at the school with her daughter, who was a peer counselor. "There was just across-the-board intolerance [of others]," Schnurr said.

Bullying was also cited as a factor in . . . school killings, according to a U.S. Secret Service study.

Several witnesses, including the aunt of slain Columbine student Isaiah Shoels, testified that Principal Frank DeAngelis had discounted their concerns about bullying. Several parents also testified that students and others were unwilling to come forward with their stories for fear of retaliation.

In fact, bullying was also cited as a factor in subsequent school killings, according to a U.S Secret Service study. Concern about bullying has prompted at least 16 states to adopt legislation recommending or requiring schools to institute programs to help kids unlearn bullying behavior. . . .

Bullying in high school has a different name, says Ralph Cantor, the Safe and Drug Free Schools Coordinator for the Office of Education in Alameda County, Calif. "It's called harassment," particularly when it has sexual overtones, he says, and a "hate crime" if it involves bullying based on sexual orientation. . . .

Jaana Juvonen, a psychologist at the University of California, Los Angeles (UCLA) who studies school culture, says bullying "may be particularly problematic in American schools." According to student surveys, she says, U.S. schools rank roughly on a par with those in the Czech Republic as among the least friendly in the Western world.

Some experts say American culture in some ways may condone, or even support, abusiveness as an acceptable way to get ahead—and not just on the playground. . . .

Studies even confirm that school bullies are often star athletes or class leaders, popular with students, teachers and administrators who are often reluctant to discipline them. "Classmates are not keen to affiliate with a bully, but they recognize that these people have social capital and power," Juvonen said. Others say the enormous size of today's public schools may contribute to the problem by providing long, unmonitored hallways or stairwells where vulnerable students can be victimized with impunity. And some teachers and parents may be reluctant to intervene—perhaps unintentionally encouraging the practice by their inaction—either because they see bullying as a natural part of childhood or because they fear adult intervention will exacerbate the situation. According to Juvonen, teachers intervene only about 10 percent of the time. . . .

But even if bullying doesn't escalate into horrific Columbine-level violence, both the victims and the perpetrators suffer in other, less-obvious ways, along with society as a whole. Bullying not only begets depression and suicide but also serious crime, researchers say, not to mention poor academic performance, truancy and higher dropout rates. . . .

People who were bullied as children are more likely to suffer from depression . . . and the bullies themselves are more likely to engage in criminal behavior later in life.

Although much is being done to reduce bullying, many parents say their children's schools are not responding quickly or aggressively enough. "I called everyone I thought could help me, and I just couldn't get it stopped," said the father of a boy who says he was bullied from the age of 12 until he dropped out of high school at 16. "It's like my son didn't matter." . . .

Bullied Kids Strike Back

Before Columbine, few Americans would have drawn a connection between bullying and schoolyard massacres. But as Gerald Newberry, director of the NEA's [National Education Association's] Health Information Network points out, "The kids who pulled the trigger weren't who we thought they were. They were not the bullies—they were the kids who had been bullied. That's what changed the focus of the schools and the nation."

In the next several years, gun-related school killings occurred in Conyers, Ga., Fort Gibson, Okla., Santee, Calif., New Orleans, La., and Red Lion, Pa. Suddenly a nationwide debate was raging over the causes and consequences of bullying on the victims, perpetrators and even bystanders.

A Bureau of Justice Statistics survey found that 86 percent of high school students said teenagers resort to violence in school because of "other kids picking on them, making fun of them, or bullying them." The Secret Service's National Threat Assessment Center and the Department of Education found that in two-thirds of 37 school shootings over the last 25 years the attackers had felt "bullied, persecuted, or injured by others" before the attack and that the bullying was often "longstanding and severe."

The findings strongly suggested that bullying could no longer be considered just a relatively harmless phase that children must go through to get toughened up for life. "Being bullied is not just an unpleasant rite of passage through childhood," says Duane Alexander, director of the NICHD [National Institute of Child Health and Human Development]. "It's a public health problem that merits attention. People who were bullied as children are more likely to suffer from depression and low self-esteem, well into adulthood, and the bullies themselves are more likely to engage in criminal behavior later in life." . . .

Yet, there are still those who think adolescent bullying is necessary for children to learn to make it in a tough world. [Ralph] Cantor, the Safe and Drug Free Schools program coordinator in California, says, "I've heard parents—usually the male parents—say, 'People just need to toughen up some. I went through this, and I've just got to teach my kid to defend himself.'"

Parry Aftab, executive director of WiredSafety.org, a group that combats online bullying, agrees that the attitude is common. "You often hear, 'Big deal; all of us were bullied,'" Aftab says. "Americans have this sense that they're supposed to be tougher. The country has a macho mindset." . . .

The bullies . . . were more likely to smoke, drink alcohol and get poor grades.

In April 2001, the first large-scale national survey of bullying in U.S. schools among students in grades six through 10 was published. Conducted before Columbine, it found that bullying was a problem that needed immediate nationwide attention. "This is a serious problem that we should not ignore," Tanja Nansel, an invesigator at NICHD and the lead author of the study, said. "In the past, bullying has simply been dismissed as 'Kids will be kids,' but the findings from this study suggest that it should not be accepted as a normal part of growing up."

Profiles of Bullies and Their Victims

Nansel and her colleagues found bullying hurts both bullies and the bullied. Victims of bullies are lonely and have trouble making friends; they are five times more likely than their peers to be depressed, bullied boys are four times more likely than their peers to be suicidal, and girls eight times more likely, according to the study.

The bullies, meanwhile, were more likely to smoke, drink alcohol and get poor grades. Most troubled of all were those who had both been bullied and had bullied others: They not only reported being lonelier and having more trouble making friends but also did poorly in school, smoked cigarettes and used alcohol. The negative effects of bullying can last a lifetime, Nansel says. "Your junior high and lower high school years are when you develop your identity," she says. "When people get the message during those very important years that they're not worthwhile, it certainly makes sense that it can have lasting effects. Similarly, for the bullies, if you learn that the way you gain enjoyment or pleasure is by doing something hurtful to another person, that's a very dangerous thing."

Indeed, society at large suffers from bullying. According to the NICHD, nearly 60 percent of boys who were bullies in middle school had at least one criminal conviction by age 24, and 40 percent had three or more convictions. "Bullying is an early warning that bullies may be headed toward more serious antisocial behavior," says Sanford A. Newman, president of Fight Crime: Invest in Kids, a crime-prevention organization of more than 2,000 police chiefs, sheriffs, prosecutors and crime survivors.

Principals feel that they're under such pressure to deliver on academics that they don't have time to deal with bullying.

Bullying also can affect school attendance, academic achievement and dropout rates. The National Association of School Psychologists (NASP) found that fear of being bullied may keep as many as 160,000 students out of school on any given day. And those who go to school are often too upset to concentrate. . . .

Prevention Programs Can Reduce Bullying Behaviors

There is considerable resistance to anti-bullying programs in many states and school districts, but nonetheless, many have joined with parents to fight bullying, and some programs have been running for three and four years. "When I first started working on bullying five years ago, I used to hear from schools and parents that the bullying issue was blown out of proportion, but I haven't heard that in a long time," says Gaye Barker, coordinator of the NEA's National Bullying Awareness Campaign. "Now everyone is talking about the issue, and almost every state—if not every school district—is dealing with it. There are always going to be some groups that are slower to respond than others." . . .

[Some] blame deeper cultural forces, specifically a society that seems to condone or reward rudeness and/or abusiveness by successful people.

"In fact, fewer than one in four schools has any real bullying-prevention programs," says Sanford Newman of Fight Crime: Invest in Kids. "It's clear that not enough is being done. There are still 3.2 million kids being bullied each year in America and 3.7 million who are bullying other children." . . .

"Principals feel that they're under such pressure to deliver on academics that they don't have time to deal with bullying," says psychologist [Ronald G.] Slaby, who is a senior scientist at Health and Human Development Programs, an educational research organization in Newton, Mass. He has been studying bullying since the mid-1980s and has developed the widely used bullying-prevention program Aggressors, Victims and Bystanders, "[Principals] don't fully understand that academics suffer if you don't have a safe, bullying-free school. Even if you are only interested in academics and not the child's welfare and freedom from violence, you would do well to have bullying-prevention programs in the school." . . .

However, some religious groups, as well as lawmakers and school officials, say that parents—not the government or schools—should be worried about disciplining and training children. And in some states, conservative Christian groups have sought to derail efforts to pass anti-bullying bills, arguing that when schools teach kids to tolerate classmates' racial, religious and sexual-orientation differences, the schools condone homosexuality and infringe on Christian kids' free-speech rights to oppose gay behavior. . . .

[According to former teacher Derek Randel of Wilmette, Ill.,] "In some very affluent neighborhoods, the schools take a 'We don't want to get the parents mad at us' approach. Frankly, many of these parents are dysfunctional parents and by bringing that dysfunction into the schools they're ruining the schools. I've seen a number of lawsuits brought by parents whose kids have been disciplined for bullying. You almost have to feel sorry for the schools, which then have to defend themselves." . . .

A Culture of Rudeness and Fear Demands Vigilance

Some experts blame bullying on the changes that have transformed society over the last few generations. For example, the anonymity provided by modern schools—often featuring large, unmonitored common areas—is frequently cited as a major reason bullies feel they can get away with abusive behavior. And the extra demands that education-reform measures have imposed on teachers often keep them too busy to be monitors. . . .

Others blame deeper cultural forces, specifically a society that seems to condone or reward rudeness and/or abusiveness by successful people. In some "reality" television shows, for instance, those who shout at their peers and are the most manipulative and backstabbing are often the ones who triumph.

Indeed, teenage bullies are often the most popular kids in school, according to a study published in 2003 in *Pediatrics*. After surveying students and teachers in ethnically diverse urban schools, the researchers concluded that teenage bullies—contrary to some stereotypes—"do not feel depressed, anxious, or lonely" because they enjoy "high social status within their peer collective." But classmates would rather not spend time with them, the survey found, indicating that perhaps "the social prestige of bullies is motivated in part by fear."

However, the authors continued, "When bullies are considered the 'coolest,' bullying behavior is encouraged"—underscoring the need to address bullying as a systemic problem that involves the entire school community. . . .

Many children and adolescents who become bystanders to bullying don't know what to say or do to stop the abuse.

Other research has found that comprehensive, schoolwide, anti-bullying programs are most effective when they raise the awareness of how bystanders contribute to the bullying problem and aim to change peer dynamics that encourage the practice. "Even when bystanders simply provide an audience of onlookers, they indirectly support bullying by providing the public acceptance that supports its perceived legitimacy and importance," researcher [Ronald] Slaby wrote. In a recent study, bystander peers were present in 88 percent of childhood bullying episodes, but a bystander intervened in less than one-fifth of the cases.

Many anti-bullying programs, such as County Attorney [James] Backstrom's in Minnesota, focus on teaching bystanders the importance of intervening, and how to do it. Many children and adolescents who become bystanders to bullying don't know what to say or do to stop the abuse. Or they may be reluctant to break a perceived "code of silence" or fearful of becoming victimized themselves. In some schools, bullies and their supporters directly intimidate bystanders into silence by stating, "snitches get stitches," according to Slaby. . . .

[Betty] Davidson, [a] former North Carolina school board member whose son was bullied, advocates continual vigilance. "There are all sorts of reasons for tuning into this problem, because ultimately we will pay for it in some fashion if we don't. It's just the right thing to do: If a kid reaches out for help, we have to try to reach back."

Masculine Defenses Are Obstacles to Healthy Expressions of Emotional Pain

Pat McGann

Pat McGann is the communications director for the Web site MenCanStopRape.com.

I have written good press releases before, but for the life of me I couldn't get a handle on how to write one in response to the recent acts of violence against girls and young women perpetrated by two males, one in a Colorado high school and the other in an Amish school in Pennsylvania. The initial draft was a muddled hybrid of intentions and possibilities, an op ed trying to be a press release, which made it bad on both counts.

Basically, it seems I find it hard to write a press release when I'm feeling mournful, sad, pissed off, and overwhelmed. In late September [2006] the *Washington Post* ran a story on the killing of three teenagers in Washington, DC within a 24-hour period, something Police Chief Charles Ramsey couldn't recall ever happening. Around the same time, there was a news story of the gang rape of a young woman in Wisconsin by two men in an alley and a third man, a cook from a restaurant, who came out the back door and joined in, taking pictures and groping her. And there was the story about the 15-year-old shooting his principal at a Wisconsin high school. Then the story about the Colorado high school. Then the story about the Pennsylvania Amish school. And in the Metro section of the *Washington Post* on October 6 [2006], a story about a Prince Georges County woman being murdered by her one time boyfriend after a judge denied her a request for a peace order because no threats or acts of violence had occurred.

Pat McGann, "The Pa. And Co. School Shootings: Press Releases and Men's Pain," October 11, 2006. http://mencanstoprape.com. Copyright © 2006 Men Can Stop Rape. Reproduced by permission.

In response to these acts [of] violence, I wanted to write more than a press release could contain, which made writing a clear and concise piece for the press difficult. Fortunately, I had help getting our message out to the media; other staff members were able to take what I had written and give it a more definitive shape. Now that the release is out, I want to write about what I couldn't include in it.

Males Aren't Taught How to Deal with Emotional Pain

I knew that after tragic incidents like those named earlier, the media wants to present the public with answers, and it seemed probable that none of the answers would clearly identify traditional masculinity as a culprit. But I didn't want to just stay on the surface of manhood; I wanted to burrow underneath to get at its muscle and bone. I wanted to write about how men's pain gets transformed into men's anger, because it seemed to me that some deep-seated anguish was underlying all the bullets, the ropes, the knives. We men typically aren't socialized to handle pain in healthy, constructive ways. Instead we're taught to "suck it up" and "get over it," which might be useful strategies some of the time but not as everyday practices—especially when it comes to violence.

Men's denial of, and removal from, their own emotional and bodily pain results in the denigration of the pain of the other.

In many of the violent incidents I was struck by the number of men who committed suicide. At the end of the Pennsylvania and Colorado school shootings both men shot themselves, as did the murderer of the Prince Georges County woman. And supposedly the Wisconsin shooting took place because the student had been bullied by students and neither teachers nor the principal would act to stop it. In each of these instances, it seems likely to me that some deep-seated, chronic despondency was present and fueled by anger, the likely source of the violence. I don't mean to suggest that the root cause of men's violence is always despair and sadness; everyone can probably clearly point to some examples of brutal acts by men that could be traced back to something other than emotional anguish, but to overlook despondency as a possible cause some of the time misses a revolutionary opportunity.

Yes, revolutionary. I'm making what could be construed as an inflated claim, but I don't think so: men dealing with their pain in responsible, constructive, and healthy ways would make the world shudder and shake, shifting the foundations of our realities. Once the dust settled, we would be in a better place, a less violent place. . . .

While women often receive encouragement . . . to deal with emotional suffering, it has yet to be normalized for men.

Repressed Anger or Hurt Can Result in Abuse

Men's denial of, and removal from, their own emotional and bodily pain results in the denigration of the pain of the other; within the logic of the masculine field, this justifies the other's oppression. Men's awareness and acceptance of their pain, then, can potentially serve as a means to disassemble the hierarchical differential between those who are supposedly "painless" and strong, and those who are "pain-full" and weak.

This is dense, theoretical language wiped clean of the ache that surges through the blood. It doesn't capture lived experience. I know because I spent years covering up emotional aches. After I married, my partner and daughter started receiving the brunt of that cover-up. I didn't physically harm either of them, but I spent a lot of time at home yelling. My daughter, never one to hold back, let me know she didn't like it. My partner wasn't too crazy about it, either.

So I worked on the yelling and anger in various ways, until ultimately, I found myself in a deep pit of pain that had nothing to do with the two of them and at times felt like it would consume me. It had built up over years and confronting it sometimes seemed like it would take more strength than I had. But eventually I came out on the other side. And when I did, my yelling slowed down and then diminished to a trickle.

My masculine defenses were so intact that for the longest time I couldn't give myself permission to acknowledge the pain. While women often receive encouragement—both in the form of popular culture and people they know—to deal with emotional suffering, it has yet to be normalized for men. In an October 8, 2006, *Parade Magazine* "Women's Health Special" article on "6 Ways To Have More Energy," number four is "Feel to heal." The section presents dealing with grief, resentment, and sadness as a necessary part of women's everyday lives; denying these emotional states grows the feelings' power and perpetuates their life, or in the words of Dr. Christiane Northrup, the author, "What we resist persists." The only related *Parade* article I could find for men appeared in June of 2004 and focused on depression in connection with a survey on men's health. Rather than a normal part of life, depression is a medical condition that we think of as limited to persons diagnosed with it, and in fact, in the survey, 61% of the male respondents thought women were more likely to suffer from it than men. Many of the other articles on men's health in *Parade* cover topics like testosterone, sperm potency, physical exercise, and prostate health.

Emotional Health Can Eliminate Brutality

All of the above topics are important, but so is men's everyday emotional health. So when we feel violent or angry, we have to find the strength to get underneath our masculine defenses and take a look at what's there. If it is pain, we have to be willing to step into it and find healthy ways to move through it. And we have to realize we can't do it alone. We need the support of the people in our lives, men and women. And they in turn need our support.

We as men have to learn how to better deal with our pain for our own well-being, for the well-being of boys, and for women and girls' safety. We have to do a better job of dealing with our pain to stop the brutal acts of violence like those in Wisconsin, Pennsylvania, Colorado, and in every community in every country every day. We have to confront our emotional life because acknowledging and dealing with our pain allows for the revolutionary possibility that we will be better able to recognize and empathize with others' pain. For all these reasons, we have to find the strength to sometimes say to ourselves and others, "It hurts."

Violence on TV and in Movies Desensitizes Youth

Suzanne Chamberlin

Suzanne Chamberlin is a senior writer and editor for Family Research Council, where she drafts commentary for both print and radio on topics such as life, media and entertainment, homosexuality, religion, education, and other issues that affect the institutions of marriage and family.

The majority of children's programming does not teach kids what most parents would prefer they learn. With only 14 percent of the networks' schedules devoted to children, young people often resort to adult programs that, more often than not, feature adult topics such as violence, drunkenness, and promiscuity. Even amidst shows devoted solely to children, such as cartoons, violence is the most pervasive element. According to the *Education Consumer Guide*, the incidents of violence on primetime television occur five times an hour, whereas the level of violence in Saturday morning programs is about twenty to twenty-five acts per hour. As the documentary *TV, Violence, and Youth* suggests, "Violence is a major course in TV's curriculum."

Not including the latest statistics [as of 2002] from the "reality TV" explosion, children will be subjected to and affected by over 8,000 murders and 100,000 other acts of violence by the seventh grade, according to a study by the American Psychological Association. A *Washington Post* article suggests that evidence from over 3,000 research studies, spanning three decades, shows that the violence on television influences the attitudes and behavior of children who watch it.

Psychologist Brian Wilcox suggests that the proliferation of cruelty and brutality on television has the following effects:

Suzanne Chamberlin, "Violence and Promiscuity Set the Stage for Television's Moral Collapse," *Insight*, June 2002. Copyright © 2002 News World Communications, Inc. All rights reserved. Reproduced with permission of *Insight*.

Copy-Cat Violence

Some viewers will tend to directly imitate or copy aggressive behavior seen on television.

- On April 25, 2001, three young daredevils raced a car toward their friend who stood in the middle of a deserted Kentucky road. The boy, who was told to jump out of the way at the last possible second, was unable to move in time. Video cameras mounted on the car dashboard captured footage of the teenager bouncing off the hood after the automobile slammed into him. Doctors marveled that the boy survived, suffering a broken leg and internal injuries. The teenagers later admitted they were repeating a stunt they had seen on MTV's *Jackass*.
- Borrowing a phrase from the latest reality game show [*The Weakest Link*], Christopher Bishop sent a bomb to his wife in July 2001, with the message, "You are the weakest link, Goodbye," on the package. The bomb did explode, giving Tracy Kilgrow-Bishop minor burns.
- In October 1993, a young girl was killed in a mobile home fire that was set by her five-year-old brother, who had been watching the lead characters on *Beavis and Butthead* meddle in pyrotechnics.
- One six-year-old boy wearing a turtle costume stabbed a friend in the arm for not returning a borrowed toy. In another incident, a three-year-old boy picked up the family cat and swung it around his head like a Teenage Mutant Ninja Turtle hero wielding a weapon. When his mother tried to intervene, the boy said, "It's just like Michelangelo."

Exaggerated Fears

People who watch more violent television tend to believe that the world is a more dangerous and threatening place than those who watch less television.

- In Dr. George Gerbner's *TV Violence Profile*, Gerbner and others found that long-term regular exposure to television can contribute to people's sense of vulnerability, dependence, anxiety, and fear.
- Of the children Gerbner observed who watched six hours or more of television a day, most have grown up with the "mean world" syndrome. They feel a need to protect themselves and buy more guns, watchdogs, security systems, and locks compared to those who watch three hours of television or less per day.

Desensitization to Violence

Perhaps the most destructive and pervasive effect of television violence, desensitization causes viewers who watch repeated acts of violence to be less horrified by it in real life. Some may even develop a "bystander" mentality, in which real violence is considered unreal.

A study in Canada showed that two years after television was introduced to a remote city called Notel, reports of physical aggression by children increased 160 percent.

- According to author H. Featherstone in the *Harvard Education Letter*, children who watch a lot of television are less bothered by violence and less likely to see anything wrong with it. In several studies, children who watched a violent program were less quick to call for assistance or intervene when, afterwards, they saw younger children fighting.

- Leading child psychologist Dr. George Gerbner notes that children who watch violent shows are more likely to strike at a playmate, bicker, or disobey authority, and are less willing to share than those children who watched non-violent programs. A study in Canada showed that two years after television was introduced to a remote city called Notel, reports of physical aggression by children increased 160 percent.
- Researchers [Robert] Liebert and [Joyce] Sprafkin found that steady consumption of violence on television creates anti-social attitudes in all individuals and a perception that violence is the first-resort in problem solving.
- Another study by Psychologist L. R. Huesmann revisited adults who watched an above-average amount of violence on television as youths. What he found was that 59 percent of those who were interviewed as children had been involved in more than the typical number of aggressive acts later in life—including domestic violence and traffic violations.

To argue that millions of people watch violent television without becoming criminals holds as much water as the argument that not all smokers get lung cancer. As Dr. Leonard Eron puts it, "The only people who dispute the connection between smoking and cancer are people in the tobacco industry. And the only people who dispute the television and violence connection are people in the entertainment industry." He goes on to say, "Television violence affects [people] of all ages, of both genders, at all socio-economic levels and all levels of intelligence. The effect is not limited to children who are already disposed to being aggressive and is not restricted to this country."

Ironically, the entertainment industry is congratulated for reducing, and in some cases eradicating, the presence of cigarettes in movies and television. In that instance, producers admitted that glamorizing them gives the wrong idea to children. But, as [author and editor] Gregg Easterbrook points out, the glamorization of firearms, which is far more dangerous, continues.

> *If the audience sees an act of violence committed by an ordinary person (in place of an actor), they are more likely to feel capable of attempting something themselves.*

Reality TV Is Violent

Unfortunately, the rash of so-called "reality TV" has intensified the debate over television violence and promiscuity. While a wealth of research has proven dramatized violence to be harmful, few studies have measured the consequences of violent programs that represent—or purport to represent—the real world.

To discuss violence in "reality TV," it is important to first recognize the range of reality genres:

- News which excludes newscasts, but includes news magazines and news interview shows such as *Meet the Press* or *Good Morning America*;
- Tabloid news shows such as *Hard Copy*;
- Entertainment news such as *Entertainment Tonight* or *Access Hollywood*;
- Entertainment non-news shows such as *Real World, Temptation Island*, or *Unsolved Mysteries*;
- Competitive game shows such as *Survivor* or *Who Wants to Be a Millionaire*;
- Police shows such as *Cops, Top Cops*, or *Real Stories of the Highway Patrol*;

- Documentary programs such as *Animal Kingdom* or *A&E Biography*;
- Talk shows such as *Jerry Springer* or *Geraldo*.

The definition of televised violence for reality programs is the same as it is for fictional programs with one exception—in reality TV, any verbal recounting of violent threats or acts are also considered in research. Previous studies have revealed that while fictional programs usually depict visual violence, reality programs tend to orally describe or report on violence instead.

Research Findings

The most prominent analyses of reality TV violence to date have been produced by the University of Texas. There the National Television Violence Study (NTVS) Research Team studied over 494 "reality" programs in the 1995–1996 season. In one year, researchers saw a 26 percent increase in the number of reality shows alone. Five years later, the amount of such programs had doubled. Their subsequent findings are as follows:

- *How much time is devoted to violence in reality programs?* Very little, according to NTVS, only two minutes of violence per show. Police programs, on the other hand, devote five times more of their broadcast to violent sequences than the average reality show. More than half of the sequences aired visual violence instead of verbal descriptions of violence.
- *What demographic is typically involved in violent sequences?* Over 70 percent of the perpetrators and victims in reality television programs were aged twenty-one to forty-four. The team also notes that a majority were of African-American descent.

- *Which weapons are typically used in reality TV's acts of violence?* Most programs show visual violence sequences involving guns, with shootings as the most common form of violence, punching and fighting ranks second. Teenagers are the most likely to use knives and commit sexual assaults. Yet for all of the police show research, NTVS recorded only one instance in fifty-three segments in which an alternative to violence was presented.

The Impact of Reality TV Is Great

Not only are there more reality shows these days and an even bigger reality show following, the violence—related content has skyrocketed. And, although relatively few research projects have focused on the American reality television phenomenon, what evidence there is suggests that realism as a feature of these shows heightens involvement, arousal, and aggression. . . .

If the audience sees an act of violence committed by an ordinary person (in place of an actor), they are more likely to feel capable of attempting something themselves. What these shows communicate to the viewer is much more deadly than the desensitization dilemma of the last three decades. Instead, the reality shows perpetuate a feeling of invincibility—which is far more dangerous than an audience that is merely less affected by violence. It breeds an "if ordinary people can do it, then I can" mentality. Meanwhile, those "ordinary people" are equipped with a number of physical and emotional safety nets unavailable and unknown to the viewers watching at home.

In other words, their televised lives are devoid of the inevitable consequences their audience would experience in duplicating what they have seen. "Real," yet sanitized.

Public Schools' Prohibition Against Teaching Principles of God Results in a Violent Society

Josh Greenberger

Josh Greenberger is an "expert author" for Ezine Articles, an online publishing site.

To say that school violence has increased over the last few decades would be a gross understatement. What has changed is not just the incidents of violence, but, most dramatically, their severity and brutality. Whereas a disgruntled student of, let's say, the '60s might have started a fist fight and, if he were really violent, used chains or brass knuckles, today's disgruntled student can take his discontentment to the extreme of the wanton killing of fellow students, teachers, and anyone who happens to be in proximity to ground-zero of the carnage.

Why? What has happened in the last few decades that would account for such a sharp decline in the behavior and moral fiber of our youth?

If you listen to some of the proposed "solutions," you get the impression that the problem is merely one of "kids falling through the cracks," and resolving the problem is as cut-and-dried as putting some rules into place, much as you would in a prison system: "Put metal detectors at the entrance to schools," "Punish more severely those who bring weapons to school," "Punish parents who don't keep guns locked up," "Have cops patrol school halls," and the "solutions" go on and on. But are these really solutions?

Josh Greenberger, "School Violence," *Ezine Articles*, January 6, 2006. http://ezinearticles.com. Copyright © 2007 EzineArticles.com. All rights reserved worldwide. Reproduced by permission.

Back in the '50s and '60s, were any of these "solutions" in place? Absolutely not. Yet, the kind of extreme violence we see in schools today was virtually unheard of then.

What has changed?

Violence on TV and in the movies? Hardly likely. War movies were one of the hottest things in the fifties—but students didn't generally come to school packing hand grenades and machine guns. Cowboys and Indians, and violent Westerns in general, were also extremely popular in the '50s and '60s—but you didn't hear of students scalping each other.

Media influence, although probably a factor, just doesn't appear to account for the steep decline in student behavior and general moral decay.

Today . . . the values of society have declined so drastically that the very basic, fundamental concept of God is seen as religion.

What has changed is society's attitude toward the values this country was founded on. Despite the fact that Thomas Jefferson called for "separation of Church and State," our founding fathers saw fit, and obviously not contradictory, to have every courtroom display the phrase "In God We Trust." All our money carries the same phrase. Why? Isn't this in direct contradiction to our founding fathers' principles? And the contradiction is so striking and obvious that it's difficult [to] imagine that it never crossed the minds of those who inaugurated it.

And if it did cross their minds, what were they thinking?

Perhaps they were thinking that the simple concept of God didn't have all that much to do with religion. What, you say? God has little to do with religion? How do you figure that? Let's see if we can explain it this way. Does doing a few laps in a pool make you a good swimmer? It depends on who you ask. If you just learned to swim, your instructor will probably call you a good swimmer. If you ask someone who trains Olympic athletes, unless you're really exceptional, he's more likely to call you a slow boat to nowhere. The analogy is simple. The moral values of earlier generations were such that the simple belief in God did not make you a religious person. Religion usually involved a host of rules, rituals, customs and/or ceremonies. Without them, you couldn't really claim to have religion in your life; you were simply a believer in God.

Today, on the other hand, the values of society have declined so drastically that the very basic, fundamental concept of God is seen as religion, is it?

The problem with all the "solutions" . . . is that they were not in place years ago, yet we had nowhere near the severity of violence then as we have today.

The fact is many scientists, after delving into the complexities of our universe, have come to the realization that there must be a Creator. Does this make them religious people? Not at all. After discovering some mind-boggling phenomenon, scientists seldom sit around talking about Santa Claus or Bar Mitzvahs. But they have been known to indulge in reflections of a Creator. Apparently, religion is religion, "God" can be arrived at logically, quite independently from religious dogma.

Although a belief in God may be the first step in becoming a religious person, just as learning to swim may be the first step in becoming an Olympic swimmer, that first step, in and of itself, does not make you a religious person or an Olympic athlete.

And this is what, I'm convinced, our founding fathers were thinking. Bringing "In God We Trust" into courtrooms and inscribing the phrase on our currency in no way goes against the grain or gist of the principles our country was founded on, and certainly not against the constitution. If our government were to start telling us when we should or shouldn't eat meat or when we should or shouldn't make Bar Mitzvahs, that would be fusing "Church and State." But simply acknowledging that there must be a God, that's not religion by any standards. That's just as much of an intellectual outgrowth of the human thought process as acknowledging that if it's raining there must be clouds up above.

We must put "God" back in our classrooms.

Now, what does all this have to do with school violence?

The problem with all the "solutions" of locking up guns, more cops, more security devices, more severe punishment, etc., is that they were not in place years ago, yet we had nowhere near the severity of violence then as we have today. And even if we were to implement many of these "solutions," there are only so many cops to go around, budgets will never allow every school to always have every security device, and, the bottom line is, you will never be able to watch every student every minute of every day.

But, wait, there is a device that's very cheap and can keep an eye on every student every minute of every day. It may not necessarily completely eliminate all violence, but it certainly can reduce its severity and incidence, as it has done very well in the past. This device was in virtually every public school in the fifties, yet it's been banned from schools in recent years. This "device" is "God."

Giving kids a conscience can, and has, and does in many communities, greatly reduce violent behavior. I can just hear it now: "But God is religion, and public schools are run by the State." Nonsense. God is not religion; after you believe in God, there's still a long way to go to religion. I know of no mainstream religion that would consider you a religious person if all you believed in was God.

We must put "God" back in our classrooms, and in grades as low as kindergarten. This is our only hope of reverting to previous, less violent times.

And for those who will still argue that God is religion, which of course it is not, and that it is "unconstitutional," I say this: It is unconstitutional to hold people against their will, but we do it to jurors regularly so they can render a just verdict. We hold kids in school against their will, in the interest of giving them an education. Martial law is also unconstitutional, but during natural disasters we routinely institute curfews to keep people from looting or rioting.

You may have the right to remain an atheist, but that doesn't give you the right to deny your kids the opportunity to grow up as decent human beings.

In the interest of saving lives and families we can certainly push aside—legally, as we do in other case—an issue which, at best, does not contradict constitutional requirements and, at worse, perhaps it does, but is perfectly acceptable in favor a greater benefit to society.

Teaching kids that if they kill or steal they will be held accountable is not a constitutional issue. It's the law. And the notion of including God as one of those who will hold them accountable, doesn't suddenly turn a civil issue into a religious one. It merely adds another dimension to the mandates of a civil society.

I must concede, however, that to teach kids in public schools about God from any particular religious perspective would, in my opinion, infringe upon their religious rights and would be unfair to their desires to stick to their own religious views. But to teach kids about God in the most basic and "generic" form, in a form that's common to and agreeable with most mainstream religions, in a form that a scientists can arrive at simply by observing the universe, in a form that says nothing more than our civil laws say, this cannot be religion or an infringement upon religious views.

And anyone who can object to teaching kids about God on "principle," is only fooling themselves—they have no principles. If "principles" are more important to anyone than human life and kids growing up as decent human beings, such a person doesn't deserve to live among human beings. To say that you have the "right" to remain an atheist is like saying you have the right to remain uneducated and ignorant. You may have the right to remain uneducated and ignorant, but that doesn't give you the right to take your kids out of school. By the same token, you may have the right to remain an atheist, but that doesn't give you the right to deny your kids the opportunity to grow up as decent human beings, and it certainly doesn't give you the right to deny those who might get killed through violent student behavior life itself.

There's no glory in the "freedom" to live in fear.

Ironically, not teaching kids about God is *not* giving them a "choice." For people who were never taught about God when they were kids, God becomes a foreign concept, not a "choice." It's only when you teach kids about God early on in life that you give them a real choice—God becomes a realistic, viable option. And if they choose not to incorporate it in their lives, well, then they've truly made their own decision.

I think "God" and some basic issues of "right" and "wrong" should be made mandatory in every public school, over all objections, in the same way that we overrule objections to other matters in the interest of a greater good for the community at large. And we don't have to worry about, "If we allow this, then the government will start running our lives in other ways." Nonsense. We have similar "unconstitutional" mandates in many areas of our lives, but we still have a live and vibrant democracy in this country. We had more rules, restrictions and mandates on our personal behavior 50 years ago and perhaps even more than two hundred years, and not only did we have a democracy then but those days were a foundation for the great nation we have today.

We have to start realizing that "democracy" is not just some play on words. It was intended to give everyone the right to live as he or she pleases, while still conforming to rules that make for a coherent and civilized society. When our constitution starts giving the impression of infringing upon our civil liberties, that is, when we become frightened of something as fundamental as sending our kids to school, then it's time to clarify the true intent of "separation of Church and State." And if it doesn't satisfy everyone, perhaps we need to go as far as amending the constitution to declare that the concept of God by itself does not constitute religion.

Either way, we have to make our laws work for us, not against us. There's no glory in the "freedom" to live in fear. True freedom comes from giving people true choices, not from concealing them. Guns don't kill. Kids don't kill. A complete breakdown of the sanctity of human life—that kills.

Current Controversies

Chapter 3

Will Stricter Gun Control Laws Reduce School Violence?

Chapter Preface

An increase in violent crimes across the nation, especially in regard to school violence, has fueled an emotionally charged gun control debate. Proponents of gun control claim that a ban on all guns is needed to eliminate gun-related crimes and deaths, especially since many guns are stolen and young children are often the victims of accidental gun fatalities. They argue that the world is simply a safer place without guns. Those who oppose gun control point to the U. S. Constitution as the instrument that guarantees citizens the right to bear arms and protect themselves; they further point to a lack of moral values as the cause of violence, not guns. Somewhere in the middle, a third group advocates for a compromise that will address the concerns of all individuals, including education about firearm safety and strict regulation of the purchase of guns.

While some believe that guns should be used just for hunting or target practice, others view any type of gun ownership as opening the door to violence and mayhem, and potentially bringing out the worst in humans. Former Attorney General Ramsey Clark stated that purchasing guns for self-defense is "anarchy, not order under law—a jungle where each relies on himself for survival." Such statements reflect the opinion that law and order is a collective responsibility, not an individual one. This line of thinking is reflected in historian Garry Wills's insistence that "every civilized society must disarm its citizens against each other. Those who do not trust their own people become predators upon their own people."

This philosophy is reflected in England's gun laws. Historically, guns have been banned there, and citizens are encouraged to retreat instead of fighting back, to rely on the community for assistance. This strategy differs markedly from what many in England have labeled "America's vigilante values," a mindset that allows citizens to defend themselves. The policy makers in England have believed that the safety of its people would be enhanced if there were fewer private guns in circulation. U.S. Supreme Court Justice Lewis Powell agreed, attributing England's low rate of violent crimes to the fact that "private ownership of guns is strictly controlled."

Opponents of gun control argue that England's approach leaves law-abiding citizens at the mercy of criminals who are confident that citizens cannot fight back. Since 1954, violent crime has been climbing in England. In December 2001, London's *Evening Standard* reported that armed crime, with banned handguns the weapon of choice, was "rocketing." From April to November 2001, the number of people robbed at gunpoint in London rose 53 percent. In that year, a person's chance of being mugged in London were six times greater than in New York.

Gun control opponents argue that there is no evidence, in England or the United States, that gun control reduces the crime rates. Michael I. Krauss, professor of law at George Mason University, points to the state of Maryland as an example. Maryland's superintendent of police refuses to grant "carry" licenses to individuals who want to carry guns, excepting politicians and celebrities. However, Maryland's crime rate is considerably higher than surrounding states that allow individuals to carry concealed weapons.

Abigail A. Kohn, a medical anthropologist and the author of *Shooters: Myths and Realities of America's Gun Cultures*, asserts that the gun control debate will go nowhere. Gun enthusiasts view gun control measures as steps toward eventually confiscating all guns, and they have no interest in making any type of deals or compromises that will lead in that direction. Kohn maintains that distrust and hostility on both sides of the debate are the elements that will prevent any type of compromise. Gun owners are unlikely to consider any type of gun control because they "don't need to consider it," states Kohn.

"For the most part, at least on the national level, they now hold the winning hand. Why tinker with success?" Kohn believes that gun owners should be open to new ideas for reasonable and effective programs that actually reduce crime and violence, and she urges gun control advocates to "give up the goal of disarming the American people."

Against this backdrop of concerned citizens with different philosophies on how best to reduce gun violence in America, particularly in schools, the following chapter examines the complexities in finding a middle ground when both supporters and opponents of gun control are vehemently convinced that their side of the debate is the correct one.

Current Gun Laws Are Weak and Ineffective

Daniel R. Vice

Daniel R. Vice is a staff lawyer for the Brady Center, a nonprofit organization that advocates gun control laws.

The National Rifle Association [NRA] has publicly claimed for years that we just need to "fully enforce existing federal gun laws," rather than "[p]assing new gun laws." Yet the NRA's actions reveal this claim to be utter hypocrisy. For more than three decades, the NRA has consistently and systematically worked to undermine and hamstring the Bureau of Alcohol, Tobacco, Firearms and Explosives (ATF) and to weaken enforcement of federal gun laws.

The NRA has also ridiculed and chastised the law enforcement officers who enforce our gun laws. It has branded law enforcement officers as dangerous "agents wearing nazi bucket helmets and black storm trooper uniforms" who "harass, intimidate, even murder law-abiding citizens." While blasting law enforcement, it has sought to protect gun law violators, even granting one rogue gun dealer—Sanford Abrams, whose Baltimore gun shop was caught committing 900 violations of federal gun laws—a seat on its Board of Directors.

The NRA Weakens Gun Laws

After Congress enacted the Gun Control Act of 1968—prohibiting gun sales to felons, the mentally ill, and children—hardliners succeeded in taking control of the NRA with the goal of opposing any form of "gun control." Under its new leadership, the NRA worked tirelessly to roll back the vital

Daniel R. Vice, "Executive Summary and How the NRA Has Undermined Gun Law Enforcement," *The NRA: A Criminal's Best Friend*, October 2006, pp. 1–2, 3, 9–11. www.bradycenter.org. Copyright © 2006 Brady Campaign to Prevent Gun Violence. Reproduced by permission.

Gun Control Act and restrict enforcement of federal gun laws. The NRA's first major success in weakening the Gun Control Act occurred in 1986, when Congress repealed crucial elements of the Gun Control Act and enacted new restrictions that severely weakened the ability of ATF to crack down on illegal gun sales.

Through the late 1980's and early 1990's, law enforcement and gun violence prevention advocates worked to enact the Brady background check law, to provide a crucial tool to enforce the Gun Control Act by identifying illegal gun purchasers through background checks on purchasers at licensed gun dealerships. The NRA strongly opposed the Brady Law, and after enactment of this law in 1993, it launched a massive effort in the courts to strike it down. At the same time, the NRA attacked the [Bill] Clinton Administration for its alleged failure to enforce the very same law the NRA was working to eliminate, stating: "It's a moral crime for [President] Bill Clinton, [Vice President] Al Gore, [Attorney General] Janet Reno and a host of Federal officers and prosecutors to fail to enforce the law. It's evil. And when innocent blood flows, it's on their hands." The NRA's claims notwithstanding, the Brady Law has been a tremendous success, blocking over 1.2 million gun sales to felons, stalkers and other prohibited buyers.

The NRA Has Support from the White House

Looking forward to the prospect of a [George W.] Bush presidency, the NRA in 2000 bragged, "If we win we'll have a president . . . where we work out of their [sic] office." After President Bush's election, numerous government and public interest group reports criticized the Administration's failure to enforce gun laws, with Brady Law enforcement actions increasing by only a miniscule 0.1% over the Clinton administration and most other gun laws almost completely unenforced. Yet with its ally in the White House refusing to enforce most gun laws, what the NRA once claimed was a "moral crime" and a reprehensible "evil" was now not even worth mention. The NRA revealed its "enforce the laws" claim to be merely political rhetoric to be discarded with the changing political winds, abandoning such claims when it meant criticizing an administration working with the NRA to repeal and undermine the very laws the NRA had claimed should be enforced.

Indeed, the NRA has never criticized President Bush for his administration's shocking failure to enforce nearly all of our federal gun laws. Rather, the NRA has worked with its allies in the Bush Administration to critically undermine gun law enforcement, through actions such as enacting a new law and regulations requiring the destruction of Brady background check records that had been used to retrieve illegal firearms from dangerous criminals and domestic violence abusers.

The Department of Justice has identified gun shows as "a forum for illegal firearms sales and trafficking."

The NRA is now pushing for new federal legislation to make it virtually impossible to enforce federal gun laws against rogue gun dealers like its lawbreaking Board Member Sandy Abrams. The NRA is also backing a bill to restrict ATF's ability to use its own records to solve gun crimes and legislation that would aid the spread of gun show sales to gun traffickers. . . .

Gun Shows Are a Criminal's Haven

There are more than 4,000 gun shows every year in this country—largely unregulated arms bazaars held in communities around the nation where the public is able to purchase firearms from both licensed and unlicensed sellers.

The Department of Justice has identified gun shows as "a forum for illegal firearms sales and trafficking" and has warned that law enforcement investigations "paint a disturbing picture of gun shows as a venue for criminal activity and a source of firearms used in crimes." It further found "a wide variety of violations occurring at gun shows and substantial numbers of firearms associated with gun shows being used in drug crimes and crimes of violence, as well as being passed illegally to juveniles." A 1999 ATF review of 314 investigations at gun shows found more than 54,000 firearms diverted to criminals. A shocking 20% of these investigations involved violations of the National Firearms Act, which regulates highly dangerous weapons including fully automatic machine guns and silencers. . . .

Furthermore, under the Brady Law, only licensed gun sellers are required to conduct background checks. Unlicensed sellers are exempt from this requirement. The Department of Justice has found that some unlicensed sellers even advertise this fact, proclaiming, "No background checks required" to would-be gun show buyers.

[The Columbine school shooters] went from private dealer to private dealer, and bought a semiautomatic assault rifle and two shotguns.

Not surprisingly, unlicensed sellers who sell guns to buyers at gun shows without keeping any records or conducting background checks are a significant source of crime gun diversion. . . .

School Killers Obtain Their Firearms from Colorado Gun Shows

In April 1999, Eric Harris and Dylan Klebold shot and killed 12 students, a teacher and themselves, and wounded 23 other students, in a shooting rampage at their school, Columbine High School, in Littleton, Colorado. They were armed with semiautomatic assault weapons and sawed off shotguns and fired 188 shots at fellow students and teachers, shooting many of their victims multiple times.

Harris and Klebold were both under age 18, the minimum age under federal law to buy a rifle or shotgun from a licensed gun dealer. They recruited Robyn Anderson, an 18-year-old Columbine High senior, to help them buy their firearms. . . .

The three then went to the Tanner Gun Show in Adams County, Colorado. . . .

They went from private dealer to private dealer, and bought a semiautomatic assault rifle and two shotguns with cash. Klebold and Harris also bought an assault pistol from a private seller who had also purchased it at the Tanner Gun Show.

Authorities later found that Harris had described his plan to purchase firearms in his journal, writing, "If we can save up about $200 real quick and find someone who is 21+ we can go to the next gun show and find a private dealer and buy ourselves some bad-ass AB-10 machine pistols. [C]lips for those things can get really f---ing big too."

Following the Columbine shootings, Congress considered legislation to require extending the Brady background check requirement to all sales at gun shows. The NRA strongly opposed the legislation. The Senate passed the legislation in 1999 when Vice President Al Gore cast a tie-breaking vote, but NRA allies successfully prevented passage of the legislation in the House of Representatives. The following year, Colorado voters passed a ballot initiative requiring background checks at gun shows in their state.

Gun Control Laws Can Reduce the Incidence of Violent Crimes

Abigail A. Kohn

Abigail A. Kohn is an anthropologist and writer.

When it comes to rancorous debates in which the two sides routinely talk past each other, gun control ranks up there with abortion and the death penalty. Last year Abigail A. Kohn, an anthropologist trained at the University of California at San Francisco, bravely waded into this battle with *Shooters: Myths and Realities of America's Gun Cultures* (Oxford University Press). A sympathetic portrait of gun enthusiasts in Northern California, the book ends with a plea for a calmer discussion of guns and crime....

A New Type of Gun Debate Is Needed

Although the Justice Department has practically promised that guns are off the national agenda, state and local gun controls affect millions of Americans. While gun owners have powerful allies such as the Justice Department and the U.S. Court of Appeals for the 5th Circuit, which in the 1998 case *U.S. v. Emerson* found that the Second Amendment guarantees an individual right to armed self-defense, gun control supporters maintain strongholds in the country's biggest cities. Having John Ashcroft [former U.S. attorney general] or Alberto Gonzales [former U.S. attorney general] on their side doesn't do supporters of gun rights much good in cities such as New York, Chicago, and the District of Columbia, where it is difficult or impossible to legally keep guns for self-defense. And

Abigail A. Kohn, "Straight Shooting on Gun Control: A Reason Debate," *Reason*, May 2005. Copyright © 2005 by Reason Foundation, 3415 S. Sepulveda Blvd., Suite 400, Los Angeles, CA 90034. www.reason.com. Reproduced by permission.

such cities may be the places where owning a gun for self-defense is most important, particularly for people who live in high-crime neighborhoods.

Given that neither side of the gun debate is going to concede defeat, and given their loathing for each other, I'd like to offer several suggestions for moving the debate forward. I come to these suggestions after several years of anthropological research on gun enthusiasts in the San Francisco Bay Area during the late 1990s. I met shooters at ranges, gun clubs, competitions, and gun shows, where thousands of Bay Area shooters regularly brave the hostility of their local government and their neighbors to enjoy their chosen shooting sports. My research educated me not only about how gun owners think and feel about their guns but also about the assumptions that both sides of the gun debate bring to the table. Until gun control supporters and gun enthusiasts re-examine some of their assumptions, neither will get far in achieving policies that are likely to reduce violence, the stated objective of both sides.

Insulting, ridiculing, or attempting to shame gun owners leaves them even more disgusted by the idea of gun control.

Guns Are Here to Stay

Here's what gun control supporters must do to have any hope of being heard on the national level again:

Stop trying to destroy the gun culture. There are more than 250 million guns in public circulation in the U.S. They cannot be wished away. Even if the U.S. government banned gun ownership and stopped all gun manufacturing and importation, it would still need to confiscate all those weapons. Doing so would require wholesale violations of Fourth Amendment rights. The probability of getting rid of guns in America, therefore, is practically zero.

Then there are the people who own all those guns. The gun culture is a multilayered, multifaceted phenomenon made up of diverse, complex subcultures. Contrary to popular stereotypes, members of the gun culture are not all potential terrorists, unemployed skinheads hanging out at gun shows, or menacing warrior wannabes in camouflage gear. Not every gun owner is a member of the National Rifle Association [NRA], in fact, some gun owners dislike the NRA. Gun owners come in all colors and stripes: They are police officers, soldiers, farmers and ranchers, doctors and lawyers, hunters, sport shooters, gun collectors, feminists, gay activists, black civil rights leaders. Most of the shooters I know are normal members of their local communities. They have regular jobs; they go to neighborhood picnics and PTA [Parent Teacher Association] meetings; they have children and grandchildren. They interact with their co-workers, bosses, employees, neighbors, friends, and families in socially positive ways. . . .

Stop demonizing gun owners. Insulting, ridiculing, or attempting to shame gun owners leaves them even more disgusted by the idea of gun control. Gun control advocates and social critics have rarely missed an opportunity to describe gun owners as "gun nuts," "gun crazies," or even "potential terrorists." If gun control advocates are only trying to rouse the passions of people who already agree with them, they may be accomplishing their goal. But presumably there is an audience sitting on the fence, an audience that includes gun owners who are open to persuasion by a reasonable point of view. Gun control supporters underestimate the ways their rhetoric alienates this reachable group of people. . . .

Use local gun owners as a resource. There are more than 75 million gun owners in the U.S. Chances are that most supporters of gun control are well-acquainted with at least one person who owns a gun and considers him or herself a gun enthusiast. Instead of relying on letters to the editor in the national press or sound bites from the NRA to explain gun enthusiasm or pro-gun ideology, perhaps gun control supporters should simply ask their friends and neighbors. If people begin honest dialogues with others they are predisposed to trust, they might be less inclined to take a hard-line position in the broader gun debate. . . .

Give up on dead-end gun control proposals. . . . [An] example of counterproductive gun control is discretionary carry permit laws, which give police the authority to decide who should be allowed to carry firearms. Such laws penalize the poor and disenfranchised, battered women, even gay activists—people whose applications police are likely to reject. By contrast, politicians and local celebrities (who often have well-armed bodyguards anyway) usually have no problem getting permits. Amazingly, such laws are still proposed as solutions for cities plagued by gun crime, where the citizens most often denied permits tend to be the ones most vulnerable to crime. These poorly thought-out policies don't just anger gun owners, they discredit the very notion of gun control. . . .

And why would gun owners want to get behind any kind of gun control policy? Because gun control is not going away. Despite the lack of evidence, many Americans continue to believe that gun control will prevent gun violence, or at least reduce it. As long as there are guns around, there will be people who insist on controlling them. No matter how effectively gun owners demonstrate their safety consciousness, or how often they use guns to defend themselves, there will always be gun control supporters who genuinely believe that owning guns causes crime. . . .

We need to start thinking about gun control as an attempt to control the black market in firearms.

That being the case, the strongest position gun owners can take is to look long and hard at the laws on the books and decide how they can be improved. Gun owners should start thinking proactively and constructively about how they can contribute to a body of law that continues to respect their rights but more effectively prohibits dangerous and criminal gun use, gun dealing, and firearms trafficking. These are the kinds of crimes (the latter two in particular) that are rampant in areas of the nation where gun control laws are strictest. Gun owners should lead the way in championing laws that address these problems. . . .

Rethink what is meant by "gun control." Until now, gun control has largely been about attempting (generally unsuccessfully) to reduce or eradicate gun crime by controlling legal access to guns. Licensing and registration, bans on "assault weapons," discretionary licensing laws: These are the defining aspects of the contemporary gun control paradigm. Instead we need to start thinking about gun control as an attempt to control the black market in firearms. . . .

Shooters can help police these problems. In any given community, gun enthusiasts are often quite familiar with the dealers who are not always scrupulously careful about selling only to legal buyers. . . .

Dirty dealing and gun trafficking don't just provide literal weapons to violent criminals; they provide rhetorical weapons to the gun control movement, which never misses an opportunity to stick it to gun owners. If gun trafficking and gun crime increase, anti-gun crusaders will turn the spotlight to the most obvious "cause" of the problem: the legal gun-owning community. Shooters should remember their own stake in ridding the community of gun crime; it benefits them in every way to get more proactive about reducing crime. Gun owners need to work assertively within the system to accomplish change that ultimately benefits everyone, simultaneously demonstrating their willingness to compromise. Accordingly, shooters need to:

Support effective violence-reduction policies. A number of projects developed in the last several years show great promise in reducing youth violence, gang activity, and gun crime generally. . . .

All the youth involved in the [Boston Gun Project] . . . (and in the community) witnessed what happened to those violent individuals, which helped deter further violence. Ultimately, the Boston Gun Project was credited with helping reduce the youth homicide rate in Boston by nearly two-thirds in the late 1990s. The project received numerous community and national awards for quality and innovation in law enforcement and policing.

It would be difficult to replicate these results without adequate funding, police support, and a community willing to make a strong commitment to its underclass. But this is the kind of program that gun owners in communities across the country should be seeking out and supporting. It jibes with the best ideas that shooters shared with me about reducing violence: better law enforcement, recognition that crime is not simply a matter of guns, programs targeting the people most likely to harm themselves and others, and working with individuals who have appropriate expertise for reducing crime. This program also could easily be considered part of effective gun control: The project discovered dealers who were engaged in illegal practices, attempted to disrupt gun trafficking, and sought to reduce or stop activities associated with gun violence.

The gun debate may not be entirely over, but shooters have an increasingly strong edge. Certainly they should be aware of the foolishness going on in places such as San Francisco [to ban all guns], and they might even consider a boycott of Pizza Hut [their delivery staff can't carry guns for protection] if that's how they want to make their point. But more important than that, they should be actively engaged in promoting a better understanding of why violence occurs. They should be seeking out programs that reduce it, leading the way in this good fight. That is how they can really win the gun debate.

Individuals Can Mobilize Others to Affect Gun Safety Laws

Children's Defense Fund

Children's Defense Fund, founded in 1973, is a private, nonprofit organization devoted to improving children's lives.

The latest data from the U.S. Centers for Disease Control and Prevention [CDC] show that 2,827 children and teens died from gunfire in the United States in 2003—one child or teen about every three hours, nearly eight every day, 54 children and teens every week.

- 1,822 were homicide victims
- 810 committed suicide
- 195 died in accidental or undetermined circumstances
- 2,502 were boys
- 325 were girls
- 1,554 were White
- 1,172 were Black
- 553 were Latino
- 51 were Asian or Pacific Islander
- 50 were American Indian or Alaska Native
- 378 were under age 15
- 119 were under age 10
- 56 were under age 5

Children's Defense Fund, "Protect Children Not Guns," 2006. www.childrensdefense.org. Copyright © 2006 by Children's Defense Fund. Reproduced by permission.

In addition to this horrific child death toll, four to five times as many children and teens suffered non-fatal bullet wounds.

More Sobering Statistics

The number of children and teens killed by gun violence in 2003 alone exceeds the number of American fighting men and women killed in hostile action in Iraq from 2003 to April 2006.

The number of children and teens in America killed by guns in 2003 would fill 113 public school classrooms of 25 students each.

In 2003, 56 preschoolers were killed by firearms. In the same year, 52 law enforcement officers were killed in the line of duty.

The number of children and teens in America killed by guns in 2003 would fill 113 public school classrooms of 25 students each.

More 10- to 19-year-olds die from gunshot wounds than from any other cause except motor vehicle accidents.

Almost 90 percent of the children and teens killed by firearms in 2003 were boys.

Black children and teens are more likely to be victims of firearm homicide. White children and teens are more likely to commit suicide.

The firearm death rate for Black males ages 15 to 19 is more than four times that of White males the same age.

A Black male has a 1 in 72 chance of being killed by a firearm before his 30th birthday. A White male has a 1 in 344 chance of being killed by a firearm before his 30th birthday.

In 2003, there were more than nine times as many suicides by guns among White children and teens as among Black children and teens.

Males ages 15 to 19 are more than eight times as likely as females that age to commit suicide with a firearm.

Young Children, Teens, and Guns

Although there has been a decline in child gun deaths since the peak year of 1994, children and teens are still twice as likely as adults to be victims of violent crime and are more likely to be killed by adults than by other children.

The vast majority of firearms used in accidental shootings of children and teens come from the victim's home or the home of a relative or friend.

The rate of firearm deaths among children under age 15 is far higher in the United States than in 25 other industrialized countries *combined.*

Since 1979, gun violence has snuffed out the lives of 98,588 children and teens in America. Sixty percent of them were White; 37 percent were Black.

The number of Black children and teens killed by gunfire since 1979 is more than 10 times the number of Black citizens of all ages lynched in American history.

The number of children and teens killed by guns since 1979 would fill 3,943 public school classrooms of 25 students each.

Since 1993, when CDF [Children's Defense Fund] launched its campaign to protect children against gun violence, the death rate of children and youth by gunfire has declined from almost 16 a day to just under eight a day. This is still a morally obscene statistic for the world's most powerful country, which has more resources to address its social ills than any other nation.

What You Can Do to Keep Children and Teens Safer from Gun Violence

It is up to adults to protect children from firearms in our homes, schools, communities, and nation. We can:

1. Support Common Sense Gun Safety Measures. The legislative record on gun safety is mixed but more bad than good. Congress continued to ignore the expiration of the 1994 Federal Assault Weapons Ban and also enacted a gun manufacturers' immunity bill that gives an unprecedented legal pass to the gun industry for liability in firearm injuries and deaths. The bill will take most lawsuits by victims of gun violence off the table. Thanks to the efforts of common sense gun safety advocates in the Senate, however, Congress passed a measure that requires child trigger locks with the sale of handguns. Now, Congress must enact legislation that closes the gun show loophole by requiring criminal background checks on those who purchase guns from unlicensed gun dealers.

Protest and refuse to buy products that glamorize or make violence socially acceptable or fun.

Stay informed. Contact your elected officials to express your views on the need for gun measures to protect children. Call the White House at (202) 456-1414 or your members of Congress at (202) 224-3121. To learn how your members of Congress voted on this and other important issues, go to the *2005 CDF Action Council Nonpartisan Congressional Scorecard* at http://www.cdfactioncouncil. org/scorecard2005.pdf.

2. Remove Guns from Your Home. A November 2004 study in the *American Journal of Epidemiology* reported that, regardless of storage practice, type, or number of domestic firearms, the presence of guns increases the risk of homicide and suicide in the home.

The vast majority of firearms used in accidental shootings of children and teens come from the victim's home or the home of a relative or friend. A 2004 study published in the *Journal of the American Medical Association* concluded that state safe gun storage laws helped achieve an 8.3 percent decrease in suicide rates among youth ages 14 to 17 years.

3. Foster a Climate of Nonviolent Conflict Resolution in Your Home, Children's School, Congregation, and Community. America is becoming a society where family violence is epidemic, child abuse and neglect are widespread, and children are being raised on TV programs crammed with scenes of brutality.

Gangs, drugs, and gun dealers are available to children 24 hours a day, seven days a week.

Concerned parents should organize nonviolent conflict resolution support groups in their congregations, schools and communities. Some excellent resources include: Dr. Deborah Prothrow-Stith's *Peace by Piece: A Guide for Preventing Community Violence*, based on the experiences of more than 40 exemplary programs across the country, and *Violence Prevention Curriculum for Adolescents*. The Association for Conflict Resolution provides a comprehensive list of educational resources for conflict resolution at http://acrnet.org/resources/index.htm. This list includes the CDF recommended curriculum, *Resolving Conflict Creatively*, created by Linda Lantieri, co-author of *Waging Peace in Our Schools*.

4. Monitor the Television Programs Your Children Watch and How They Use the Internet, and Don't Buy Them Violent Video Games. Write to advertisers who sponsor violent television shows and sell violent electronic products to children. Talk to your children about the need to reject violence as a cultural and personal value. Protest and refuse to buy products that glamorize or make violence socially acceptable or fun.

5. Help Focus Public Attention on Child Gun Deaths. Each year, encourage the reading of the names of children in your community killed by guns at your place of worship; publish their photos in your congregational bulletin. Urge local newspapers and radio and television stations to publish and broadcast photographs of children and teens killed in your community. Write a letter to the editor or an opinion column about the tragic loss of young lives to gun violence, and take other steps to raise awareness of violence against children.

6. Engage in Child Watch Visitation Programs. Visit hospital trauma units and support the families who have lost children. Educate others about the human and financial costs of gun injuries. There are four to five nonfatal firearm injuries for every gun death of a child or teen. In addition to the enormous toll these injuries take on the lives of those affected, the annual health care costs are in the billions of dollars. A 2004 study in the *Journal of the American Medical Association* reported that gunshot injuries in the United States add up to $2.3 billion a year in lifetime medical costs of which about half is borne by taxpayers.

Boston's innovative and collaborative strategy resulted in a nearly 67 percent drop in youth homicides.

---

7. Provide Children Positive Alternatives to the Streets So They Can Feel Safe and Protected. Gangs, drugs, and gun dealers are available to children 24 hours a day, seven days a week. What positive competition for their attention is available in your community? Make your schools and places of worship venues of quality summer and after-school programs. Check CDF's Web site at http://www.childrensdefense.org for more information about CDF Freedom Schools reading and service model, which includes nonviolence training.

8. Organize a Ceasefire Initiative in Your Community. Gun violence is out of control in many American communities, particularly poor, urban neighborhoods. But some cities are addressing the problem by organizing programs modeled on Boston's successful Ceasefire initiative, which became known as "The Boston Miracle." Ceasefire brings families, faith groups, social service providers and the police together to halt the killing of teens by other teens. Boston's innovative and collaborative strategy resulted in a nearly 67 percent drop in youth homicides. At the heart of the Ceasefire approach is the belief that we are all responsible for what happens in our communities and that young people, given the opportunity, will choose a path away from violence. But to do so, they must have resources and caring adult support. Ceasefire programs are operating in a dozen communities across the country. For more information about beginning a Ceasefire initiative in your community, contact David Kennedy, Director, Center for Crime Prevention and Control, John Jay College of Criminal Justice, dakennedy@jjay.cuny.edu or (212) 484-1323....

Gunshot Deaths: What One Surgeon Sees

The grim realities behind gunshot death statistics are even more depressing when seen from a frontline urban hospital trauma center. Dr. Edward Cornwell, Professor of Surgery and Chief of Adult Trauma at Johns Hopkins University Hospital in Baltimore, sees dozens of gunshot victims each year. In 2005, the hospital's Level 1 trauma center booked 88 deaths, mainly from penetrating wounds—gunshots or stabbings. Most of the victims were Black male teenagers. Sixty-one were dead on arrival (DOA).

Victims of gunshot wounds and stabbings between the ages of 15 and 24 make up 70 percent of the center's trauma patients. Since Dr. Cornwell came to Johns Hopkins in 1998, major steps have been taken to upgrade the trauma center with resources that would enable it to improve its record in saving the lives of gunshot victims. More lives have been saved among patients with blunt injuries from motor vehicle crashes and serious falls.

About half of the victims who do not die from bullet wounds have head injuries so severe that they are brain dead.

Yet, there have been no improvements in the number of lives saved among gunshot victims. In fact, according to Dr. Cornwell, while the number of assaults in Baltimore remains unchanged, the number of shooting deaths has gone up. "I've seen a disturbing increase in the number of deaths caused by a single gunshot at close range to the head or chest. What's most alarming," says Dr. Cornwell, "is the high volume among these instant fatalities of youths under the age of 21. In one week last year, on each of five consecutive nights, we saw a 20-year-old DOA. All of them were shot in the head or chest."

About half of the victims who do not die from bullet wounds have head injuries so severe that they are brain dead. The few survivors often undergo multiple surgeries, followed by intensive care and long courses of physical therapy and medication.

Dr. Cornwell is unapologetically blunt about condemning what he sees as some of the major causes of Baltimore's gun violence. The easy availability of guns is high on the list. He also blames what he calls the city's "broken school system," noting that "60 percent of the Black men who go to jail are school dropouts. An overarching contributor to gun violence," he says, "is popular culture that condones underachievement and glamorizes brutality." Dr. Cornwell is angry as he describes the futility in stitching up a teenager with 15 stab wounds who had "Thug Life" tattooed on his forehead and "Kill or Be Killed" across his chest. "We saved his life, but he's going to be dead in five weeks or five months," he states. "This has got to stop because it's tearing at the fabric of our communities across the country."

People, Not Guns, Are the Problem

Craig Medred

Craig Medred is the "Outdoors" editor and an opinion columnist for the Anchorage Daily News.

Once more a tragedy is fueling those now old arguments about the U.S. Constitution's Second Amendment protection of the right to keep and bear arms.

Americans love guns or fear them.

At the pier on this island off Maui, you could see both—the gun lovers toting their cased shotguns from the ferry toward the shuttle bus that would take them to a popular shooting clays range; the gun nervous eyeing the gun cases as if they might contain weapons that would jump out and begin shooting on their own.

Away from the pier later—sitting in the shade of the deadly, cancer-causing tropical sun—I read a *San Francisco Chronicle* columnist ranting on how America would be a better place if guns were simply banned. It was a piece obviously not written by someone who once shot a grizzly bear off their leg to ensure the damage would end just above the ankle.

Evidence of Gun Violence Is Over-exaggerated

There is, obviously, no arguing with the contention that banning guns from this country—if that were possible—would eliminate gun deaths.

Craig Medred, "Look, People, Guns Are Not the Problem, We Are," *Anchorage Daily News*, April 29, 2007. www.adn.com. Copyright © 2007 *The Anchorage Daily News*, a subsidiary of The McClatchy Company. Reproduced by permission.

Likewise, there is no argument that banning motor vehicles would eliminate motor-vehicle deaths.

Motor-vehicle accidents killed about 43,000 people—5,000 of them innocent pedestrians—in 2005.

About 30,000 people died from guns in the same year, more than half of them intentionally. Suicide is a horrible thing for the family and friends of the victim, but it is not something of concern to any of us in society at large.

Homicides—one person shooting and killing another—numbered about 12,000.

Cars Are More Dangerous

Given the numbers, you can see the chances are about three times better you'll be killed by someone driving an automobile than someone wielding a gun. Not only that, the stranger who kills you—if you are so unlucky—is far more likely to be the driver of another automobile than someone wielding a gun.

This whole argument about gun control distracts from the real issue in this country, which is a national epidemic of rage.

Given these realities, we would clearly be safer if we banned cars than if we banned guns.

But all of this is also open to all kinds of speculation and differing interpretation. As has been observed before, there are liars, damn liars and statisticians.

You can make almost any argument you want on this issue, and the residents of the virtual world are doing that now.

Virginia Tech Shooting

The latest tragedy at Virginia Tech [where a student shot and killed 32 people on April 16, 2007], one side argues, might have ended with only a few people dead if there had been an armed citizen on the scene to shoot it out with the killer.

The latest tragedy at Virginia Tech, the other side argues, wouldn't have happened at all if there was better gun control, if it was hard to get a gun, if guns were banned, etc.

Both arguments are as valid as they are invalid.

No one can know what might have happened if there had been someone on the scene able and willing to stop the killer with a bullet. Likewise, no one can know if any gun law would have stopped, or even slowed, this killer's commitment to his murderous task.

The Real Weapon Is Rage

And the real problem is that this whole argument about gun control distracts from the real issue in this country, which is a national epidemic of rage.

Guns aren't bad things or good things. They're things, inanimate objects, chunks of metal with no will of their own.

In the latest case, the rage might have been fueled by mental instability, but it remains symptomatic of the rage that seems to boil just below the surface all across America.

When kids get mad at each other in Anchorage now, they don't decide to pull on the gloves and have it out in the ring; they try to kill each other.

Sometimes, too often, they use guns. Other times, though, it's knives or baseball bats or boots. The problem isn't the weapon of choice, it's the anger.

Why that is? I don't know.

Why it is isn't talked about more is equally beyond my knowledge.

Maybe it is a question too hard to address. Or maybe it is like other issues we, as a society, just don't want to confront.

Health Problems Kill More People

Look, if we really wanted to save people in this country, we would stop worrying about gun control and institute mandatory, government-enforced daily exercise.

It's a documented fact exercise improves mood, which might help people deal with some of the rage, but that's the tip of the iceberg.

The really serious death rates in America aren't tied to gunfire or automobiles, at least not directly. They're tied to lifestyle.

Consider these numbers on annual deaths from the Centers for Disease Control [CDC]:

- Heart disease: 654,092
- Chronic lower respiratory diseases: 123,884
- Diabetes: 72,815

Change Lifestyles and Save Lives

All of these are, in significant parts, what are called "lifestyle diseases." If as much time and energy was spent worrying about them as is spent fretting over gun control, lots of lives could be saved.

Even a 10 percent reduction in deaths from heart disease would save more people than eliminating all deaths from motor-vehicle accidents and firearm homicides combined. The latter deaths, of course, are impossible to zero out no matter what is done. The former is something about which we might be able to do something.

So is the flu. Flu and pneumonia, according to the CDC, kill more than 61,000 people per year.

If the people intent on trying to ban guns in this country put the time, energy and money they spend on that issue into seeing that the old, the young and the infirm got flu shots, they might be able to save more lives than they would by totally eliminating homicide by firearm.

Guns Are Things

And the reality is that banning firearms is a stupid, utopian idea. Yes, it would make the world a safer place, unless you're the guy with a grizzly bear's teeth already in your leg or a single woman confronting a man with a knife in your home.

Guns aren't bad things or good things. They're things, inanimate objects, chunks of metal with no will of their own.

They're really not the problem. We are.

We are a society in which solving problems with violence has become an almost accepted norm. Our entertainment is full of it. We celebrate gun violence on film.

And when someone acts this out in real life, we blame the gun. There is something wrong here, all right. I'm not sure it's firearms.

Teachers Should Be Allowed to Carry Guns

Dave Kopel

Dave Kopel is a research director at the Independence Institute. Founded in 1985, the Independence Institute is a nonpartisan, nonprofit public policy research organization dedicated to developing and sharing social policy ideas with citizens and government agencies.

Since the Columbine murders in 1999, several important steps have been taken to prevent or thwart school shootings. Much more still needs to be done.

The good news is that, since Columbine, police tactics in school attacks have dramatically changed. At Columbine, the armed "school resource officer" refused to pursue the killers into the building, and kept himself safe outside while the murders were going on inside. Even after SWAT [special weapons and tactics] teams arrived, and while, via an open 911 line, the authorities knew that students were being methodically executed in the library, the police stood idle just a few yards outside the library.

To this day, the authorities in Jefferson County, Colorado, have successfully covered up who made the decision that the police would stand idle.

The willingness of people to speak up has been the most significant post-Columbine step forward in safety, and has likely saved many dozens of lives.

Fortunately, police tactics have changed dramatically since that disgraceful day. Now, the standard police response to an

Dave Kopel, "The Resistance: Teaching Common-Sense School Protection," *National Review*, October 10, 2006. http://article.nationalreview.com. Copyright © 2006 by National Review, Inc., 215 Lexington Avenue, New York, NY 10016. Reproduced by permission.

"active shooter" is immediate counter-action. For example, at a March 2001 attack on Santana High School in Santee, California, the police response was immediate, and saved lives. It was the first time ever that a school shooting had been met with prompt police counter-action. . . .

Self-Defeating Self-Esteem

After Columbine, there was a great push for anti-bullying programs and the like. Whether bullying was or is a major cause of shootings is debatable. Columbine killer Eric Harris likely suffered from a superiority complex; his problem was excessive self-esteem. Indeed, many criminals have excessively high self-esteem, and one cause of their criminality is the large gap between how most people see them (accurately, as mediocre losers) and their own self-image. Self-esteem programming in the schools, whatever its merits, might even be counterproductive to school safety.

One important value of anti-bullying programs, however, is that most of them strongly encourage students to come forward and report a problem. Much more so than in the pre-Columbine period, students and other community members who hear rumors or threats of a school attack have been willing to warn the authorities. There have been many attacks which have been prevented only because someone did so. The willingness of people to speak up has been the most significant post-Columbine step forward in safety, and has likely saved many dozens of lives.

Compared to the Columbine aftermath, there is much less inclination among the political classes, and, even much of the media, to use school murders as a pretext for irrelevant anti-gun laws. If it were actually possible to ban all guns, and confiscate all of the more than 200 million firearms in America, school killers would be deprived of their most effective weapon—since most killers don't have the skills to build bombs, and a criminal can't use a knife or sword to control two dozen people at a distance.

One reason why adult sociopaths so often choose to attack schools . . . is that schools are easy targets.

But it is pretty clear that the kinds of laws which were pushed after Columbine (one-gun-a-month in California, special restrictions on gun shows in Colorado and Oregon) are of little value in keeping guns away from people who plan their attacks a long period of time in advance. . . .

The Kids Aren't Always the Killers

The attacks this fall highlight a problem that was forgotten in the post-Columbine frenzy. There are lots of attacks which are not perpetrated by disaffected students. We knew this in 1988, when 30-year-old Laurie Dann attacked a second-grade classroom in Winnetka, Illinois, and in January 1989, when an adult criminal named Patrick Purdy attacked a school playground in Stockton, California. Or when British pederast Thomas Hamilton killed 16 kindergarteners and a teacher in Dunblane, Scotland.

One reason why adult sociopaths so often choose to attack schools—schools to which they have no particular connection—is that schools are easy targets. It is not surprising that police stations, hunting-club meetings, stateside army bases, NRA [National Rifle Association] offices, and similar locations known to contain armed adults are rarely attacked.

Because of the spread of concealed-handgun licensing laws, now in 40 out of 50 states, whenever you walk into a place with a large crowd of people—a restaurant, a theater, a shopping mall—you can safely assume that several people in the crowd will have a license to carry a concealed handgun, and some of them are currently carrying.

Schools are one of the few places in the United States where the government has guaranteed that there will be no licensed, trained adults with a concealed firearm that could be used to resist a would-be mass murderer.

One confirmation of the strength of the case for allowing teachers the choice to be armed is the weakness of the arguments against it.

Since this fact is apparently obvious to random psychopaths, it would be very dangerous to assume that the fact is not obvious to terrorists also. Beslan, Russia, shows that terrorists with al Qaeda [terrorist group] connections consider schools to be good targets. There is also the danger of self-starting jihadis, such as the man who attacked the Jewish community center in Seattle. Every Jewish school and community center should very seriously consider having at least one full-time security guard.

Israel has successfully used a combination of security guards, armed teachers, and armed escorts on field trips to protect schools from terrorist attack. Thailand is likewise allowing teachers to obtain handgun-carry licenses in southern regions where schools have been targeted by Islamic terrorists.

One confirmation of the strength of the case for allowing teachers the choice to be armed is the weakness of the arguments against it. Significantly, we have real-world tests of the policy—not only in Israel and Thailand, but also in the United States.

The State Solution

Like many states, Utah enacted a concealed-handgun licensing law in 1995. Unlike most states, Utah did not make schools an exclusion zone for lawful carrying. Not only a teacher on duty, but also a parent coming to pick up a child from school, can lawfully carry a concealed handgun in a Utah school building—after, of course, passing a background check and safety training. . . .

After eleven years of experience in Utah, we now have exactly zero reported problems of concealed handgun licensees misusing guns at school, or students stealing guns from teachers, or teachers using their licensed firearms to shoot or threaten students. During this same period, we also have had exactly zero mass murders in Utah schools.

I suggest that dead students . . . are far more inconsistent with a learning environment than is a math teacher having a concealed handgun.

My proposal, however, is not that other states go as far as Utah. Rather, I simply suggest that teachers and other school employees be allowed to carry if they obtain a handgun carry permit. If a school wants to require special additional training for school carry, that's fine.

Some people who do not like the idea of teachers being armed to protect students simply get indignant, or declare that armed teachers are inconsistent with a learning environment. I suggest that dead students—and the traumatic aftermath of a school attack—are far more inconsistent with a learning environment than is a math teacher having a concealed handgun.

"Teachers don't want to carry guns!" some people exclaim. True enough, for most teachers. But there are about six million teachers in the United States, and it would be foolish to make claims about what every teacher thinks. The one thing that almost all teachers have in common is that they have passed a fingerprint-based background check, meaning that they are significantly less likely than the general population to have a criminal history.

There are plenty of teachers who have served in the military, or the police, or who have otherwise acquired familiarity with firearms. And there will be other teachers who would willingly undergo the training necessary to learn how to use a firearm to protect themselves and their students. After all, almost all the teachers in southern Thailand are Buddhists, and if some Buddhist teachers will choose to carry handguns, it would be ridiculous to claim that American teachers, as a universal category, would never exercise the choice to carry.

We know that school shootings have been stopped by armed citizens with guns. In 1997, a Mississippi attack was thwarted after vice principal Joel Myrick retrieved a handgun from his trunk. The killer had already shot several people at Pearl High School, and was leaving that school to attack Pearl Junior High, when Myrick pointed his .45 pistol at the killer's head and apprehended him. A few days later, an armed adult stopped a school rampage in Edinboro, Pennsylvania.

Defensive training for teachers can also include how quickly to disarm a person with a gun.

It is commonly, but incorrectly, believed that the federal Gun-Free School Zones Act (GFSZA) creates an insurmountable barrier to arming teachers. Not so. The GFSZA has a specific exemption for persons who have a concealed handgun carry permit from the state where the school is located, if the state requires a background check before issuance of a permit.

It is state laws, not the federal GFSZ Act, which are in need of reform to allow schools to be protected.

Your School, Right Now

Pending legal reform, there are several steps that school districts can take to improve school safety. Almost all teachers spend several days a year in continuing professional education programs. Every school district should begin, at least, offering self-defense training as an option to teachers on "in-service" days.

These programs should explain the critical importance of decisive action by teachers in the very first moments when an armed intruder has entered a room. The faster that students get out, the more lives that can be saved. Allowing an intruder to take control of the room, and line students up, or tie them up, is extremely dangerous. If students flee immediately (especially if the room has at least two exits), the criminal will have a much harder time obtaining control and taking hostages.

Undoubtedly, the criminal might begin shooting immediately. But if the victim is moving and is constantly getting further from the shooter, it is much harder for the shooter to deliver a critical hit. In contrast, when the victims are stationary and under the shooter's control, the killer has an easy time delivering a fatal head shot from a foot away. At Columbine, some fleeing students were wounded, some of them very seriously. But almost all the fatalities were the result of up-close executions of stationary victims.

Defensive training for teachers can also include how quickly to disarm a person with a gun, especially when his attention is distracted. This can be a dangerous move, to be sure, and it does not always work. If it does, perhaps everyone's lives can [be] saved. If it does not, the killer has no greater power than if the move were never attempted.

At a more advanced level, there are programs such as Krav Maga ("contact combat")—a technique of unarmed self-defense currently used by some U.S. police departments, and the Israeli Defense Forces. It was originally created by Jews in Bratislava [Slovakia], during the 1930s, for self-defense against anti-semitic thugs who might have weapons. Every school district should offer to pay half the tuition for a teacher who takes classes in Krav Maga or similar programs. Introductory versions of these programs could also be offered for free on in-service days.

Of the teachers who would never choose to carry a firearm, some would choose to carry non-lethal defensive sprays. Basic training in defensive spray-use takes an afternoon. Schools could offer more sophisticated training as well, focused on the situations most likely [to] be encountered in a school.

Pepper sprays are not always a panacea (they don't work on some criminals, especially ones who eat a lot of spicy foods), but they can save lives. While a predator is writhing in excruciating pain, he will lose control of the situation, allowing students to flee, and giving the teacher a good chance of taking the gun.

It is the policies of the pacifist-aggressives which have turned American schools into safe zones for mass murderers.

And what about self-defense for students? Incorporating several days of self-defense into the annual physical education curriculum would be sensible anyway, even if there were no problems with school shootings. Self-defense training will make students less vulnerable at isolated bus stops, and everywhere else. The core of all self-defense training is greater awareness of one's environment, so that a person can get away from potential trouble before it becomes actual trouble.

Self-defense training also teaches that it is dangerous to let a criminal take control of your surroundings; even if a criminal is pointing a gun at you, you are probably better off to try running away, than to let him put you in a car where he can transport you to an isolated location.

Teachers and students would also learn that it is sometimes better to submit; if you can surrender your purse to a mugger and protect yourself from injury, that [is] often the safe choice. We know, however, that when an armed criminal attempts to take over a school, there is no realistic hope that the criminal will be satisfied with stealing some money.

Consider a 12th-grade classroom containing 15 healthy males, several of whom are athletes. If the males rush the perpetrator en masse, some of them . . . might be shot, but it [is] also likely that the perpetrator would be quickly subdued, all the more so since most school shooters are not physically powerful. The school shooting in Springfield, Oregon, ended when several brave students, including wrestler Jake Ryker, rushed the shooter; Ryker was shot, but recovered.

To some people, the notion that teachers like Joel Myrick or students like Jake Ryker should engage in active resistance is highly offensive, and the idea that teachers and students should be encouraged to learn active resistance is outrageous.

Our nation has too many people who are not only unwilling to learn how to protect themselves, but who are also determined to prevent innocent third persons from practicing active defense. A person has the right to choose to be a pacifist, but it is wrong to force everyone else to act like a pacifist. It is the policies of the pacifist-aggressives which have turned American schools into safe zones for mass murderers.

School shootings are the ultimate form of bullying, and long experience shows that the more likely and more effective the resistance, the less the bullying.

If a trained teacher carries a concealed defensive tool, such as pepper spray, there is no downside except an offense against the self-righteous sensibilities of pacifist-aggressives. Except for criminals, everyone would be a lot safer—and not just at school—if teachers and students were encouraged to learn at least basic unarmed self-defense.

Will Alternative Juvenile Interventions Help Prevent School Violence?

Chapter Preface

"The hardest part of my job as a [New York] prosecutor," says Peter Reinharz, "is facing victims or their relatives after the perpetrator has figuratively—and sometimes literally—gotten away with murder. The philosophy behind the state's no-fault juvenile justice system might have made sense in the days when juvenile offenders stole apples and picked pockets, often driven by poverty." But violent teen criminals today should be treated as criminals, not juvenile delinquents, according to Reinharz.

Reinharz points to criminals like Keith A., who was prosecuted along with several accomplices for savagely beating a drunk in upper Manhattan's Mount Morris Park and then dousing him with lighter fluid, as he screamed and begged, burning him so badly that his charred corpse was scarcely recognizable. Keith, a couple of weeks shy of his thirteenth birthday, then went home and had a snack. Keith received a mere eighteen-month sentence. The truth, says Reinharz, is that "we have had very little success rehabilitating violent teens." He doesn't believe that experts know how to rehabilitate violent youths, and finds it hard to imagine that an eighteen-month sentence is long enough to "untangle a twisted character, to undo 14 or 15 years of bad influences and bad habits."

Attorney and author Wendy Kaminer disagrees with those who dismiss rehabilitation or advocate harsh punishments for violent teens. She claims that to do so permanently stigmatizes kids who want to rehabilitate themselves. Housing juveniles with adults is another harsh measure that Kaminer opposes. She points to statistics from the American Civil Liberties Union (ACLU) claiming that "children housed in adult prisons are five times more likely to be sexually assaulted, twice as likely to be beaten by staff, and eight times more likely to commit suicide than those sent to juvenile facilities." Kaminer also contends that racism exists in the judiciary system, which results in harsher treatment for minorities. Kaminer points to a study by the Office of Juvenile Justice and Delinquency Prevention which illustrates that while African American boys represent only 26 percent of juvenile arrests, they represent 52 percent of all children transferred to adult court.

Others, such as Deborah Shelton, MD, attribute mental health problems to teens' violent behaviors, and advocates appropriate treatment in a rehabilitation setting. She believes that "the decision not to provide treatment services to youth in need and under their [the justice system's] care implies neglect." Dr. Shelton finds it disturbing that youths who were diagnosed with schizophrenia were the least treated group. She asserts that a one-size-fits-all approach is not effective; rather, an integrated approach that includes the family, therapy, and the judicial system are more effective. As the situation is now, the mental health needs of youth are not being identified or treated.

Leslie D. Leve, a research scientist, also disagrees with punitive measures for teens. Instead, Leve advocates group care programs which focus on skill building and participation in family therapy. Leve finds juvenile facilities especially disturbing since research shows "the powerful effect that delinquent or deviant peer association can have." Research suggests that aggregation of at-risk teens produce negative effects, including negative outcomes in their adult lives. Leve supports a program that utilizes trained foster families who focus on behavior management methods, a structured living environment, close supervision, and clear rules and limits. Close monitoring of school attendance and performance, along with a psychiatric evaluation and treatment, are also necessary components of an effective program.

Society appears to be locked in a maze of confusion regarding effective treatment methods for juvenile offenders. Educators, lawyers, doctors, parents, and the average citizen all seem to promote a magical formula that will guarantee a solution for acts of teen violence. The authors in this chapter debate the need for changes that will help ensure a safer society.

Violent Youths Need Rehabilitation, Not Punishment

Peter Ash

Peter Ash is a forensic child psychiatrist and associate professor in the Department of Psychiatry and Behavioral Sciences at Emory University in Atlanta, Georgia.

When I talk . . . about criminal responsibility I'm talking about blameworthiness, or culpability. The question is the degree to which adolescents, or at least some adolescents, are less blameworthy than adults who commit similar acts. I'm not suggesting that less blame leads to their being not guilty. Rather, the question is whether certain aspects of adolescents mitigate what should happen to them in the justice system. What does an adolescent who has committed a violent act deserve? This question has received relatively little attention, but I think ideas about it nevertheless drive much of our thinking about how we actually respond to violent youth.

One reason the question of adolescent culpability has received so little attention is that since the establishment of the juvenile court in 1899, the theoretical construct driving juvenile interventions has been rehabilitation. The juvenile court isn't so interested—in theory—in punishing as in trying to get the kids better. Moral blame doesn't enter, in a significant way, into juvenile court adjudications. However, the pendulum has really swung. Now we hear, "You do an adult crime, you do adult time." The nature of the act rather than the nature of the actor is at issue. Culpability is particularly timely now because of its reference to the juvenile death penalty debate, and the juvenile death penalty, as I'm sure you know, was recently ruled unconstitutional. But similar issues are also relevant to

Peter Ash, "Challenges of Adolescence and Violence," Lecture hosted by the Center for the Study of Law and Religion at Emory University, March 23, 2005. www.law.emory.edu. Copyright © March 23, 2005. Reproduced by permission of the author.

such questions as the conditions under which a youth should be transferred to adult court, what interventions and sentences a juvenile convicted in juvenile court should receive, or what interventions and sentences a juvenile in adult court should receive.

Eighty Percent of Adolescent Offenders Do Not Become Adult Offenders

So what do we know about adolescent violence? Time does not permit me a very full discussion, but there are [a] few key points I'd like to raise for you to keep in the back of your mind as we discuss these issues. The first is that the *onset* of serious violence, and by serious violence I mean violence in which a weapon is used or someone is seriously hurt, is an adolescent phenomenon. About half the kids who will ever become violent become violent by age sixteen. If you get to age twenty-five and you have not committed a violent act, the likelihood that you ever will is extremely low. This has some interesting implications. For example, if you are talking to an adult spouse abuser and you ask the man, "Tell me when you were violent as an adolescent," and he says, "Oh, I wasn't," you can compute with about 99 percent certainty that he's lying. The second key point to keep in mind is that adolescent violence is common. Here we're working off data largely from self-report studies (studies on arrested youth give incomplete numbers). These studies suggest, depending on how they define violence, that between 30 and 40 percent of adolescents by the time they reach 17 have committed a violent act. The number for girls is about 15 to 30 percent. Almost half of the boys and a large number of the girls have committed a violent act. That is, violence is hardly uncommon in adolescence. It's a relatively typical adolescent phenomenon. The third point is that adolescent violence, for most kids, is time-limited to adolescence. Fewer than 20 percent of violent adolescents go on to be adult criminals. The fourth point I want to make is the characteristics of juvenile crime are somewhat different from those of adult crime.

We know that arrested juvenile offenders have triple the rate of mental health problems of juveniles in the normal population.

First of all, juvenile crime tends to be group based. Youths offend in groups, as opposed to adult crime where you have typically more single actors committing the crimes. Second, adolescents don't specialize, they are quite diverse in what they do. They cover the whole range of behaviors. Third, another myth many people have is that adolescent crime is race-related. Statistics suggest that if you correct for socio-economic status, the difference between white and African-American offending largely vanishes. The rates are essentially the same. This is not true, of course, of arrest rates: African-Americans are arrested at a much higher rate.

The fifth point to keep in mind is the question of how much all of this is a mental health problem. We know that arrested juvenile offenders have triple the rate of mental health problems of juveniles in the normal population. Mental health problems are extremely common in this population. However, the extent to which this causes or aggravates their violent behavior remains unclear and needs much more research. Last, I want to remind you of the recent history related to adolescent violence. In particular, there was a huge crime wave in adolescent violence beginning in the early eighties which peaked around 1993. In this period the adolescent homicide rate tripled. In 1993, for African-American urban youth, homicide was the leading cause of death. It exceeded all natural causes of death combined, including motor-vehicle accident deaths. It was a huge epidemic. This epidemic triggered a wave of great fear for public safety and led to legislative responses which were highly punitive. For example, the Georgia legislature, a little harsher than most but somewhat typical, passed what's still known as Senate Bill 440 which mandates that any youth 13 years old and up who commits one of seven violent offenses (the most common of which is armed robbery with a firearm) is automatically sent to adult court—there to receive adult punishment and adult sentences.

Since 1993, for reasons that remain unclear this crime rate has largely dropped. In the context of what's happened over the last few days, school shootings also added to the sense of danger in public and particularly at schools, but I do want to point out that despite school shootings, schools statistically are one of the safest places that an adolescent can be.

Teens and Adults Have Different Levels of Culpability

I want to turn now briefly to *Roper v. Simmons*, for which the Supreme Court announced its decision on March 1st ... [2005], which highlights this issue. The court found a national consensus against the death penalty for juveniles and said at one point: "Today our societies view juveniles as categorically less culpable than the average criminal." The court didn't give a very clear account of what went into culpability and I want to go through the argument with you in some little detail. There are essentially three main threads to the issue. The first is immaturity. Justice Stevens, writing for the majority in *Thomspon v. Oklahama* in 1988, a case in which the Supreme Court found it unconstitutional to impose the death penalty for 15-year-old defendants, said, "Thus the court has already endorsed the proposition that less culpability is attached to a crime committed by a juvenile than to a comparable crime committed by an adult. The basis for this conclusion is too obvious to require an extended explanation." Notwithstanding that it was obvious, the following year the court held that executing 16 and 17 year olds was permissible. Then finally this year [2005], of course, they found that it was not.

When the court took *Roper v. Simmons*, the professional associations became very interested in writing briefs to support a finding that the juvenile death penalty was unconstitutional. Most of the major associations, and certainly the American Psychiatric Association, already had taken as a formal position that the death penalty for adolescents was not justified....

Psycho-social maturity was a better predictor [of anti-social behavior] than age.

So what do we know about adolescent development? The first thing is that reasoning, by which I mean *cognitive* decision making, at age 15 is, by and large, similar to what you see in adults. There were a number of studies in this in the early nineties, particularly around issues such as being able to consent to medical treatment. These findings were used to support other briefs to the Supreme Court arguing that adolescents were competent to consent to an abortion without parental oversight. This finding presents something of a problem, because the associations were now trying to argue that there are ways in which there is immaturity at 15. The distinction made was that what you have in adolescence is an immaturity of judgment, a construct referred to in some of the literature as "psycho-social immaturity." It encompasses a number of components such as impulsiveness, adolescent sense of time, the relevance to the future, the ability to put oneself in another's position, and resistance to peer pressure.

Maturity and Brain Development Are Legal Considerations

[Professors Elizabeth] Cauffman and [Lerner L.] Steinberg did a fascinating study of normal high school kids in which they rated psycho-social maturity, and then they also had the youth rate how likely they were to engage in anti-social acts under a variety of conditions (they also did this with adults). What they found was that psycho-social maturity was the best predictor of how anti-social the choices would be that the child made. Psycho-social maturity was a better predictor than age. While age and psycho-social maturity tended to go together, if you're predicting whose going to be anti-social, then maturity was the better factor.

The second line of immaturity has to do with the notion that the brain is still developing. When I was in medical school, I was taught that the brain is essentially physiologically finished by age six. When I joined the faculty, they were saying that the brain develops up to the beginning of puberty. In the last five years, there has been considerable research showing that the brain continues to develop into the mid-twenties. . . .

The court looked at all the scientific briefs, and as best I could tell summed it up in one sentence that said, "As any parent knows, and as the scientific and sociological studies tend to confirm, youth are more immature." That seemed to be our effect on the case.

Certainly to the extent that circumstances outside one's control affect behavior, responsibility is reduced.

There is a problem, however, with the immaturity argument, which is, immaturity compared to what? In my job, I talk to a lot of people who have committed crimes, adults as well as kids. I can tell you that if you talk to them about what they were thinking at the time of the crime, you will not be impressed by their maturity of judgment. From a treatment perspective, if you could raise most of these adult defendants to the level of an average 15 year old you would consider this a huge therapeutic success. Since we hold adults culpable for their acts and imprison them, if decision-making capacity is all there is to blame-worthiness, once a person reaches a certain level of maturity—and that level is probably way below that of the average adult—you should be held fully culpable, although one might decide to punish differently for other reasons. . . .

Teens Have Little Control Over Their Environment or Moral Development

There are two other threads to the argument that adolescents are less culpable. The first has to do with the external circumstances the adolescent finds himself in. My lawyer colleagues tell me that for an adult, in most cases, being a product of a "rotten social background" is not helpful in mitigation. The idea is that adults, in principle, can change their circumstances. Adolescents, however, by and large cannot. You're stuck with who your parents are, you don't have a choice of school, and you don't have a choice of who the other kids are living on your block. Certainly to the extent that circumstances outside one's control affect behavior, responsibility is reduced. A critical external circumstance for adolescents is their interpersonal milieu, particularly their peer group. There are a number of developmental considerations that highlight this. The first is to remember the point that adolescent crime is much more peer-based than adult crime. So, depending on who your peers are, you are much more likely to engage in crime. Second, adolescents as a group are much less resistant to peer pressure. Third, in the culture of the street, violent responses may be a reasonable coping strategy. If you aren't prepared to use violence you may be seen as a patsy and actually be more likely to become a victim.

There's also a moral argument here which is complicated. I'm going into a philosophical realm I'm not very familiar with, but I will pose it for your consideration. It's the idea that responsibility has something to do with expectations.

Consider a group in which a lot of people smoke, and then consider another group in which very few people smoke. You are likely to think of someone in the group where most people smoke as less responsible with making an independent choice than you [are] when you judge the person in the group where very few people smoke. Blame-worthiness in some sense is related to an expectation of how people actually behave. Moral transgression should be deviant. Now recall, in this context, the frequency of adolescent violence.... Most of us think of it as rare. If you change your expectation that violence is much more common, it becomes, in some sense, less morally deviant.

We expect that at the end of adolescence the adolescent will be a different person than at the beginning.

The third line of reasoning has to do with the fact that an adolescent's character is still developing. In a case on mitigation, *Johnson v. Texas* from 1993, the Court said: "The relevance of youth as a mitigating factor derives from the fact that the signature qualities of youth are transient. As individuals mature the impetuousness and recklessness that may dominate in younger years can subside." There is a line of argument that bad acts reflect bad character. Now here we need to distinguish between at least two senses of character. The first is the sense that an act may be "out of character." The federal sentencing guidelines for non-violent crimes allow for the possibility that if a person leads a clearly blameless life, is a good citizen, and then does something that seems just out of character for that person, that unusual-ness can be taken into consideration as a mitigating factor in sentencing.

Teens' Moral Character Is Not Fully Developed

Now we need to look at adolescents. There is a developmental progression of offenses in adolescents. Adolescents do not start with a serious violent offense. They tend to start with things like minor delinquency, vandalism, progress through substance abuse, and then go to aggravated assault, which is generally a precursor to rape and other crimes of that sort. There is a developmental progression. So a serious violent offense is, unfortunately, very much in character. There's a second sense of character, though, that affects adolescents, which is that their character is not fully developed. We expect adolescents to change. We expect that at the end of adolescence the adolescent will be a different person than at the beginning. . . .

We want to allow personality to develop in a positive way, and providing adult sanctions doesn't do this. To give another example of how this argument works, my friend the philosopher Dan Hausman has suggested that as we grow older we gradually come to reflect on what we have absorbed from our environment and either endorse it or break away. As we mature we increasingly reflect on the values and customs on those around us and our responsibility grows. Someone whose moral and intellectual capacity at age 45 are less than that of most 15 year-olds may nevertheless be held more responsible because he has had an opportunity, despite limited abilities, to build his own life. Even a gifted 15 year-old, in contrast, who possesses far greater abilities, has not had the opportunity to choose a life for himself. To treat crimes committed by 15 year-olds like crimes committed by adults does not recognize that the 15 year-old has not had an opportunity to become an adult and to carry out the sort of reflection that makes his action reflect a fixed character for which unmitigated moral judgment and retribution are appropriate.

Rehabilitation Is Effective For Teens

I don't want it thought that I'm advocating that kids who do bad things should just get off. They do bear considerable responsibility for their acts. I also recognize there is more to punishment than moral transgression. Among other issues, we clearly need to maintain public safety. I am fully persuaded that there are bad kids out there from whom the public need to be protected and for whom relatively little can be done. It is instructive to look at the research, which is somewhat mixed but tends to find that if you punish adolescents with adult sanctions they recidivate at a higher rate, that is they commit more crimes after they get out, than similar youth who are treated in the juvenile system.

There are a number of implications to this. First, it is an argument for rehabilitation rather than punishment. In the 70's it was commonly held that "nothing works" with these kids. The good news is that the mental health fields have come a long way, and we now have pretty good data for interventions that are cost-effective in reducing recidivism. They're not wonderful and they don't help everybody, but overall programs such as multi-systemic family therapy, intensive supervised probation, and certain social skills training programs have been shown to be useful in decreasing later offending.

In my view, a consideration of what delinquent adolescents deserve will move us away from the punitive approaches adopted over the past 15 years towards more individualized assessments of who should receive adult punishment and more services for those youth we can help.

Preventive Interventions Need to Begin at an Early Age

Marian Wright Edelman

Marian Wright Edelman is the founder and president of the Children's Defense Fund, a nonprofit organization that advocates for all children with a special focus on the most vulnerable.

Families, schools and the juvenile justice system are failing at-risk children, making them vulnerable to the Cradle to Prison Pipeline.

Patricia Clark remembers the first time she met Frankie several years ago. Clark, chief judge for the Juvenile Division of King County Superior Court in Seattle, had to lean over slightly to see him from the bench in her courtroom. Frankie, a 10-year-old good-looking African American boy, was charged with assault stemming from an angry outburst in his foster care placement. This charge was a misdemeanor.

Anger and depression are essential elements of Frankie's makeup. He was taken from his mother at birth and spent the first eight years of his life moving from one foster home to another. As his behavior problems got worse, he was moved into therapeutic foster care so those issues could be addressed. Instead of analyzing his needs and adjusting his treatment, the therapeutic foster home where he was placed called the police after Frankie hit a staff member. He was arrested and charged—the first entry in what has become a long criminal record. The last time Judge Clark saw Frankie, he was 15 and charged with multiple felony robbery offenses. He was convicted and is now serving a three-year sentence in Washington State's juvenile prison. When he gets out, he will be 18 and

Marian Wright Edelman, "Losing the Children, Early and Often," *Crisis*, November–December 2006. Copyright © 2006 by The Crisis Publishing Company, Inc. Reproduced by permission of the publisher and the author.

will have aged out of the child welfare system. With no support or resources, his next stop will very likely be an adult prison.

Some Babies Are Destined for Prison

Frankie was failed at every turn by his parents, the child welfare system and the juvenile justice system—all the adults in his life who should have protected and nurtured him. In tragically real terms, a prison cell has been reserved for Frankie since before he could even crawl. And all of his life, he has been on a course toward that prison cell through what the Children's Defense Fund (CDF) has identified as America's "Cradle to Prison Pipeline." There are tens of thousands of children like Frankie—nearly 100,000 juveniles in detention alone—to say nothing of the children who are not incarcerated but live lives that are, at best, marginalized. They come mostly from low-income families in depressed neighborhoods and the majority of them are children of color. During their childhoods, the multiple entry points to the pipeline will seldom be far away. . . .

CDF has been researching the entry and exit points of the pipeline, talking with the families and children who are at risk, those who live in the pipeline, and also talking with advocates, service providers and others who work to dismantle it. There are four key "feeder systems" into the pipeline—healthcare, early childhood education, the foster care system and schools.

For a nation that claims to be the world's greatest democracy and a beacon for justice and freedom, this crisis is unacceptable.

Race and poverty form the foundation of the pipeline, but its multiple components include struggling families, depressed communities, underperforming schools, broken child welfare and juvenile justice systems, disparities in access to healthcare and mental health treatment and a political ethos that prioritizes incarceration over prevention and child development.

Under the nation's system of juvenile justice, poor children are arrested, convicted and incarcerated at younger and younger ages. About two-thirds of these children are locked up for non-violent offenses. One reason more children are being routed into the pipeline is the advent of zero tolerance laws in the mid-1990s. These measures led to the shuffling of many children directly from the schoolhouse to the jailhouse at the initiative of school-based police officers. . . .

For a nation that claims to be the world's greatest democracy and a beacon for justice and freedom, this crisis is unacceptable. The Cradle to Prison Pipeline must be dismantled. It costs our nation billions of dollars each year and ruins the lives of tens of thousands of our children. And the prison pipeline is sapping low-income communities of the young talent needed to build a brighter future.

Criminal Prevention Begins with Healthcare

One factor in determining whether a child enters the prison pipeline is access to healthcare. Currently, more than 9 million children in America are without health insurance, and the latest statistics show the number is growing.

Parents who struggle to provide food, clothing and shelter for their families often find it difficult to get their children to a health clinic.

A healthy start for any child begins in the womb, but many low-income pregnant women do not receive prenatal care or health counseling. Black and Latino women are more than two times as likely as White women to have late or no prenatal care. Women who abuse alcohol or drugs while pregnant are more likely to deliver low birth-weight babies. Children are placed in greater jeopardy if they don't receive routine healthcare, including the standard vaccinations against diseases such as measles, mumps and rubella.

One in five children have a diagnosable mental, emotional or behavioral disorder. Some of these problems include attention-deficit hyperactivity disorder, depression, post-traumatic stress disorder, dyslexia or mental retardation. These and other unaddressed health problems such as hearing or vision loss and learning disabilities—which can be effectively treated if caught early—often turn into deficits and developmental delays in poor children and those without health insurance.

People are often surprised to learn that an overwhelming majority of all children living in poverty—70 percent—are living in working families, usually headed by single mothers. Yet the bread-winners of these families may not receive health insurance through their low-paying jobs, so the health problems of their children often go undiagnosed until they become serious and treatment becomes more challenging. Parents who struggle to provide food, clothing and shelter for their families often find it difficult to get their children to a health clinic.

These parents also have little energy left to provide the stimulation that is critical to a child's early development, such as taking them to the zoo or a museum and reading to them at night. Teen mothers whose own education and personal development have been arrested by early pregnancies are often still learning how to be adults themselves and so are unprepared to raise a child. Children who begin their first critical years with unhealthy starts are likely to begin school not ready to learn. Unless they receive serious intervention, they may never catch up. . . .

Schools Feed the Justice System

The number of African American and Latino teachers in public schools is significantly lower than the number of White teachers and the population of public school teachers is overwhelmingly female. Poor minority children attend schools where there are few teachers who look like them and have very few male role models in the classroom. In 2001, while 90 percent of public school teachers were White, 6 percent were African Americans and the percentage of male teachers was at a 40-year low at 21 percent. It is not uncommon for teachers to have low expectations for children from marginalized families, at least in part, because administrators lack the cultural competence to relate to their problems.

Many children are locked up, not because they commit crimes, but because they have a mental or emotional disorder.

As a result, a child may be penalized for having poor English skills or may be labeled "dumb" or even mentally retarded because he has a common learning disability like dyslexia or attention-deficit hyperactivity disorder. Children may act out in school if they come from homes where they are beaten or sexually abused. Public schools are hard pressed to acquire the staff or resources to recognize these problems and provide counseling and therapeutic help for their students. It is much more likely that a child's behavior will be perceived as insubordinate, disruptive or unruly. In these cases, "zero tolerance" disciplinary standards are frequently applied.

A disturbing outgrowth of the zero tolerance approach is that schools are becoming the point of entry into the juvenile justice system as children are increasingly arrested on school grounds for subjectively and loosely defined behaviors such as "disorderly conduct" and "malicious mischief." In Miami-Dade County, Fla., for example, a 2003 report showed that student arrests had tripled since 1999. In 2004, more than 2,500 students were arrested while at school. One need only recall the 2005 case in Florida of the 5-year-old who was handcuffed and arrested by three St. Petersburg police officers for having a temper tantrum in her kindergarten classroom.

Many children are locked up, not because they commit crimes, but because they have a mental or emotional disorder. Parents who don't know how to deal with such behaviors are sometimes left with no option other than relinquishing them to the foster care or juvenile justice system, hoping that they will then get the mental health treatment they need.

Only about one-third of the juveniles in detention nationwide have committed a violent offense.

Some children are sentenced to juvenile detention facilities because they are awaiting treatment that does not exist in their communities. In July 2004, a U.S. Senate committee heard evidence that 15,000 children with psychiatric disorders were improperly incarcerated in 2003 because no mental health services were available. Sadly, we're seeing more cases where children with mental disorders from families with money get psychiatric intervention, while poor children end up with the prison psychologist. . . .

Unequal Justice for Poor Children

There are more boys in the prison pipeline, but it is open to girls, too, and they are the fastest growing population in the juvenile justice system. Among victims of abuse and violence at home, the entry offense into the prison pipeline for girls is often domestic violence. One scenario might be two sisters fighting—when one punches the other, a parent calls the police and they are taken to a juvenile detention center. The second time the police are called, one or both are charged with a felony.

To be sure, teens arrested for serious crimes—armed robbery, assault, car theft and homicide—must be appropriately accountable for their offenses. However, only about one-third of the juveniles in detention nationwide have committed a violent offense. The juvenile justice system handles more than 1.6 million cases a year. Many of them are relatively minor infractions that used to be handled by families and community organizations. With their dockets crammed, juvenile courts have become one of the biggest feeder systems of the Cradle to Prison Pipeline....

Poor children and teens who reach juvenile court often face an overcrowded system where they are unlikely to be treated fairly. A poor child charged with an offense may appear before a court with no member of his family to stand with him, and he may not understand the legal process or the gravity of the situation. His case may be assigned to a public defender whom he meets for the first time on the day of his trial. By contrast, a teenager from a family with resources will likely appear in court with both parents and an attorney. They may persuade a judge to be lenient in exchange for the family's promise to send the child to drug rehabilitation or military school.

We must all take personal responsibility to advocate for children and be change agents in our communities.

Judges pressed to process as many cases as possible often dispense verdicts in minutes. Once they enter the juvenile justice system, the chances that poor and minority children and teens will get a second chance are not good. Too few judges offer poor youthful defendants alternatives to incarceration—restitution, community service, electronic monitoring, drug treatment or placement in a "staff secure" but not locked community corrections facility....

Dismantling the Pipeline

The Cradle to Prison Pipeline must be demolished along with the structures and policies that support it. This will be a daunting task, but every segment of our society should take part in this effort. First, we must all demand that programs that work be fully funded and that policies that contribute to criminalizing children be eliminated.

We've already heard Frankie's tragic story. Frankie's needs were not met by either the foster care or the juvenile justice system—in fact, these systems only exacerbated his problems. Our society must be able to keep what happened to Frankie from happening to other children in similar circumstances.

We should start by guaranteeing healthcare coverage, including mental health treatment, for all children in America. This should be a national priority. Next, we must provide greater financial support for proven early childhood development programs that build healthy bodies and minds such as Head Start and Early Head Start. Schools must be fully funded, Zero tolerance policies responsible for mass suspensions and abusive treatment of young children must be terminated.

We must also dismantle the pipeline at home. Parents must get the help they need to become the best parents they can. We must all take personal responsibility to advocate for children and be change agents in our communities. Individuals and families can open their hearts and homes by being role models and mentors and nurturing children in need. One can join the national mentoring program Big Brothers and Big Sisters, for example. Families can set another place at the dinner table once or twice a week for an at-risk child. If you are taking your children to a museum or the zoo, make room in the car for another child. Buy an extra ticket to a ballgame or play.

Society Must Invest in Children

There are a variety of opportunities for communities to make a difference by working to keep schools open after hours as safe havens from the dangerous influences of the streets. Much of the trouble children and teens get into occurs after school and before their parents return from work, between 3 p.m. and 6 p.m. There are numerous tested model programs that partnerships of parents, educators, community organizations, pastors and local governments can come together to replicate.

We ignore the continuing devestation of the Cradle to Prison Pipeline at our peril. We must recognize that the failure to improve healthcare coverage, schools, and the child welfare and juvenile justice systems will perpetuate the cycle of criminalizing children. We must secure our future by investing in families to enable them to nurture children who will grow up to be strong, self-sufficient adults who are good parents and assets to their communities. . . .

Violence Education Classes Will Reduce Violence

Mary Paquette

Mary Paquette is editor of Perspectives in Psychiatric Care, *and is a psychotherapist in private practice.*

Thousands of studies, such as the research in [the October–December 2004] issue of *Perspectives in Psychiatric Care*, have been conducted studying aggression and violence, yet we continue to experience the tragedy of uncontrolled impulses, anger, and shame. There are numerous workshops, programs, and assessment tools for youth and adults—many have been empirically researched and proved to lower the rates of violent acts. However, we can do more to reduce domestic, school, work, and random violence in our country.

Along with teaching the facts of violence, there needs to be a raising of consciousness to facilitate an awareness of potential violence as opposed to the comfort zone of denial that violence could not happen in this family, school, or workplace. Avoidable violence can be detected and dealt with only when there is a willingness to see the potential of violence in anyone. Everyone has the potential for violence. Biologically, we are hard wired with neurological pathways for aggression necessary for survival. Under the right circumstances, everyone is capable of using violence to protect themselves from harm, to save face, or to get revenge.

The Warning Signs Are Ignored

Take a look at a tragic violent event that occurred in Santee, CA, on March 5, 2001, when 15-year-old Charles Andrew Williams killed two students and wounded 13 others. The com-

Mary Paquette, "Violence Education: Dissolving the Denial," *Perspectives in Psychiatric Care*, October–December 2004. Copyright © 2004 Basil Blackwell Ltd. Reproduced by permission of Blackwell Publishers.

munity was stunned by this event, and the familiar and pathetic refrain, "I never thought it could happen here," was voiced by students, teachers, and parents. When you try to live in a bubble of innocence, you will miss the most obvious signs of risk that a child is in trouble. Was this event avoidable? The facts speak for themselves.

It was only a matter of time until Andy would explode with the fury of humiliation.

Andy made a homemade video, which was aired by the television news magazine "Inside Edition" after the shootings. Andy expresses anger at having to move from Maryland, and shows images of his father's locked, glass-fronted gun cabinet. Andy was a pleasant and well-adjusted child in Maryland, where he was popular and well liked. He moved to California with his father, who was relocating to a new job, and was never accepted by the students at his new school.

Everyone knew his peers bullied Andy. He was picked on all the time, shoes snatched from his feet, his apartment was egged, he was jeered and taunted, his homework was ripped apart, his skateboard and money were stolen, and he was beaten up at a dance. Yet, no one realized the consequence of being repeatedly shamed is shame-rage. It was only a matter of time until Andy would explode with the fury of humiliation. His desire to take revenge would override his rational sense of right and wrong.

Andy demonstrated his sense of alienation by hanging out at Woodglen Vista Park, a cultural and social center of a ragtag, nose-ringed collection of hard-core stoners and skaters; many joined this group because they did not fit or were not welcome in any of the other social groups. He took up drinking, smoking marijuana, skipping school, and defying his 11 P.M. curfew. He was obsessed with Kurt Cobain, who committed suicide, and the punk group Linkin Park, and played over and over again "In the End . . . I had to fail/To lose it all/but in the end; it doesn't even matter."

Predictable warning signs were missed.

Andy told at least four friends and one adult that he was going to shoot up the school. Even though they may have taken him seriously, they did not check his backpack or report it to the school principal or police. Most important, the adult's response to Andy was, "You're joking, right? You'd better be joking, because if you're not, I will call the police right now." He threatened Andy rather than intervening.

Society's Denial Prevents Intervention

Predictable warning signs were missed. Tormented by his peers, Andy was alienated and running from his psychological pain by using drugs and alcohol. Andy was always clowning around, so when he boasted he was going to bring a gun to school, no one believed him. "I'm going to do it, just wait and see," had no real meaning to the four students he told about his plan to harm others. Why not? What does a kid have to do to get someone's attention—to make them realize he is at the end of his rope and out of control? What else could Andy have done, given the circumstances, to alert the community that he needed help? "It makes us ask who we are, what we did or did not do. It challenges your reality," said one distraught parent. Reality needs not just challenging, but changing.

Taking violent threats seriously requires that we come out of our denial that a scrawny 15-year-old with a sense of humor can be a murderer. Had Andy's threat been reported and knowledgeable people done a little investigating, they would have identified several risk factors present that would have resulted in a high risk for homicide. We need to learn the difference between a serious threat and an immature comment.

There are warnings, and students do not go on spontaneous shooting rampages. In 75% of school shootings, people noticed signs such as violent threats, harassing phone calls, graphic drawings, and torturing animals prior to the violent event.

Parents can do everything right and, still, some kids go haywire.

Another 15-year-old boy was arrested for making threats on the Internet that he would bring an AK-47 [assault rifle] to the school and shoot 75 students and plant bombs. Classmates also had mistreated him. His attorney said, "Her client is a good kid from a religious family and that she didn't think the threat would go that far." This statement reflects the widespread belief that coming from a "good" family protects the child from bad behavior. Many parents believe that if they spank their kids and teach them right, guns will not be abused. Parents can do everything right and, still, some kids go haywire. It is easier to be in denial than live with the uncertainty of how our children will deal with life's disappointments and difficulties. What can be done to break the denial of "this can't happen here" or "not my kid" or "he would not hurt a flea"? This is denial, and denial is dangerous.

Education Is Key in Identifying and Preventing Violence

There needs to be violence education classes in the schools, just as there is sex education. Students, teachers, and parents need to learn the theories of aggression—what makes people angry, aggressive, and violent. Everyone needs to develop a healthy respect for the profound tendency humans have to learn violence and implement it. Educate teachers, parents, and students to do a homicide assessment in the same way professionals do a suicide assessment. When a child says, "I am going to shoot people," the next question is not, "You're joking, right?" The next question needs to be, "Do you have a plan, do you have a weapon, do you have a time? What is going on that you want to do this? Sounds like you are having a hard time. Let's go to a [teacher, parent, school counselor, etc.] for help with this situation."

Research shows that the combination of shame and rage is a formula for explosive violence. We need to teach this to teachers, parents, and children. Impress on students how very hurtful their teasing and harassing can be, and the consequences of humiliating and shaming another. The outcome may be the death of themselves or their best friend.

What most people struggle with is coming out of their comfort zone of denial and realize the truth about people who perpetrate aggression on others.

Role-playing exercises in which someone is shamed slightly so they can identify their initial reaction as shame-rage can be beneficial in understanding the desire for revenge. Yes, Andy was smiling when shooting the students. He was finally feeling good after months of being shamed and ridiculed. This rage needs to be dispersed, and the most satisfying way to do this is to shame or harm someone else. Kids who ridicule other children need to experience the pain and humiliation of that in a safe, controlled environment and learn that this feeling can lead to murderous rage. Their safety at school is dependent on not shaming other students. This is a simple but powerful lesson to learn.

We Need to Acknowledge the Potential for Violence in Everyone

We teach our children not to let strangers touch them. Why not teach them the consequences of shame? Why not help them understand the phenomena of shame and countershame?

That Andy did nothing when his skateboard and money were stolen says that he was harboring a lot of rage and resentment. It was only a matter of time until they got discharged. Students, as well as teachers and parents, need to be taught to recognize shame, rage, and resentment and know the outcome will sooner or later be violence.

Education on the facts is only partially the answer. What most people struggle with is coming out of their comfort zone of denial and realize the truth about people who perpetrate aggression on others. Mostly, they are just like us—good, decent people—who under the right circumstances commit terrible acts of violence that make sense to them at the time. The willingness to see ourselves as potentially violent makes it easier to see the potential for violence in others who are like us—our loved ones, our children, our neighbors, as well as strangers. Recognizing that we are all capable of committing violent acts—sweet young children as well as nice adults—is the first step in violence prevention. We need to take responsibility for our own inner violent urges and impulses and see them in others as an expected outcome of shame and rage. As nurses, therapists, educators, and parents, we can make a difference by seeing violence where it is—right in front of us—and intervening before it is too late.

Jail Time Can Do a Child Good

Angela Neustatter

Angela Neustatter is a journalist who specializes in social and humanitarian issues. She has written extensively on matters concerning children, and is currently the editor of YoungMinds *magazine, located in England.*

Charmion Togba was not the kind of kid you'd have wanted on your patch. He says it himself. At the age of 16, he was manufacturing crack cocaine and "doctoring" guns for contacts. But that's all changed. Today he works with children at risk, and this summer he is running programmes for the Arts and Offenders' Unit Splash Extra programme, funded by the Arts Council and Youth Justice Board. Reflecting on the change, he gives a big smile: "It was prison that turned me around. I was angry, directionless and saw only a future in crime. The place I was sent treated me with decency and helped me see I could make different choices. And gave me the opportunity to develop in a way I wanted."

It's not what you expect to hear from someone locked up at Her Majesty's Pleasure while still just a child—Charmion was 17 at the time and this was his second sentence. His first sentence, at the age of 16, served at Feltham Young Offender Institution (YOI), had done nothing to improve his frame of mind: "You learnt survival of the fittest, to shut up and shut down . . . I came out more, not less, ready to commit crimes."

But his second sentence was served at Huntercombe YOI near Oxford, a place that is pinpointed by many radical thinkers on juvenile punishment as having a particularly humane and constructive ethos and regime. It startled Charmion to

Angela Neustatter, "Prison Can Be the Right Place for Kids," *New Statesman*, vol. 2, no. 12, August 19, 2002. Copyright © 2002 New Statesman, Ltd. Reproduced by permission.

find that the governor, Paul Mainwaring, had brought in musical instruments and set up a recording studio because so many inmates were keen to make music. Charmion developed his recording skills, took NVQs, [National Vocational Qualification], was given a job training other inmates. Before his release, the prison helped him get funding from the Prince's Trust to return on a regular basis and keep training inmates, "so I didn't have that terrible thing that trips so many kids up, even if they want to stay straight, of having nothing when they get out". He was also funded by the trust to start his own company, Genocis, running arts and multimedia programmes with children who risked following a similarly delinquent trajectory to his own.

If this were an isolated case, it would be risky to hold it up as proving anything. But in the course of 18 months spent talking with children—boys and girls—in six YOIs around the country . . . I was startled at how many said prison had given them something they needed and could not get outside: regular meals, a bed to sleep on, people who would listen to them, a chance to take stock of their lives and escape from a chaotic, drug-fuelled, out-of-control spiral that would have led them deeper into crime.

It may seem perverse to suggest that prison can be a suitable place for children and even a potentially positive experience.

Often they praised a particular member (or members) of staff for caring about them and giving them valuable support and guidance. Education and skills training they would not, or felt they could not, get outside proved unexpectedly appealing and opened their minds to new directions.

Youngsters like Shehwah Shah, who suffered racism and bullying, and disliked much about his three-year sentence at Lancaster Farms YOI, now consider that "going there was the best thing that could have happened to me". Why? Because this young man, whose father walked out when he was five, leaving his mother struggling to earn enough to bring up the family, with little time or energy for her children, had a personal officer who was like a dad. "He came and talked to me in my cell and he helped me see I could do something with my life. I'd been thrown out of education in prison for behaving badly, but I went back and there were two wonderful women there who gave me another chance and spent a lot of time working with me once they saw I was serious."

The result was a place at Sunderland University, from which he recently graduated with a 2.1 [a respectable grade point average], as he tells with heartbreaking pride.

Prison is what we have, and where these children will continue to be sent.

We have the grim record of imprisoning more than 10,000 children and young people (15- to 21-year-olds) each year—more than any comparable European country. Our courts are already far too quick to incarcerate child miscreants whose crimes in no way merit it. Thus it may seem perverse to suggest that prison can be a suitable place for children and even a potentially positive experience. Certainly, it runs directly counter to the beliefs of reforming organisations such as the Howard League for Penal Reform . . . and the Children's Society. The dogged and vigorous campaigning of both these organisations against the human rights abuses which undoubtedly are inflicted on children in many prisons is admirable and vital. Here we share common ground. Nor do I ignore the trenchant verdict of the former HM [Her Majesty's] Inspector of Prisons Sir David Ramsbotham, who said that what he saw of children in prison was "wholly unacceptable"—the bullying, assaults, racism, degradation, isolation and fear that are all too often their daily fare (and too often ignored and condoned while child inmates are voiceless and powerless). Such abuse can only damage children and increase the chances that they will go out and harm more victims.

But the reformers take an absolutist view—that prison is never a fit place for children. Yet around 22 per cent of crimes committed by under-21s—and often enough by children in their early and mid-teens—are violent. Sometimes hideously so. Research from the Joseph Rowntree Foundation . . . showed that, in a self-report sample of 14,000 pupils, nearly a quarter of 15- to 16-year-olds admitted carrying a knife over the past year and one in five had attacked someone intending to cause serious harm.

[The] [p]ublic and victims do not want dangerous young people running loose. Those who must be taken out of circulation, the reformers argue, should always be sent to local authority secure units, where the Children Act must be observed and child development and therapeutic approaches built into the regime.

Absolutely—in an ideal world. But let's talk reality. Keeping a child in a secure unit costs [pounds sterling] 3,000 a week compared with [pounds sterling] 46,000 a year for a child in a juvenile prison unit. There are nowhere near enough secure places and it is very unlikely, in times when the *Daily Mail's* hard line on young offenders is popularly shared, that the taxpayer will agree to greater spending on child offenders who knife old ladies, rape girls on towpaths and commit savage murders.

So prison is what we have, and where these children will continue to be sent. We should not silence discussion around the idea that these YOIs can offer children a regime that they themselves consider positive.

What is urgently needed is to find out what can change the angry and alienated hearts and minds of children, and to build their confidence and skills so that they are better able to live a constructive life outside.

An inspiring pioneering place to study is the Owen Unit at Castington YOI in Northumberland, where the staff take children who have committed the most severe crimes. It is a low-lying building with a well-tended garden. Inside, the atmosphere is relaxed, prison officers joke with trainees (they are not called inmates) and the governor, Mick Lees, speaks fiercely of the need for humanity, respect and decency because "most of these kids have been screamed at, humiliated and treated rough and it hasn't stopped them".

But until we, as a society, become more interested in the youngsters who go wrong . . . prison remains the place where they will go.

But it's not a soft option: a lot is demanded of the children educationally, and Castington has just had an impressive Ofsted [education] report. Matthew, 15, in for a nasty, violent attack and illiterate when he arrived, grins fit to break when he tells how he won a prize for a children's book he made for his sister. Donny, 17, who got life for killing a man after a drug-crazed fight, describes himself as "always a bad boy, always angry. No parent could have coped. Here they expect you to be respectful and they're good to you. I've learnt to curb my temper. They've got me to think about my victim and I wish I could go back and change what I did. I'm training to be a mechanic, learning to get up and work every day. The funny thing is, I like myself better than I ever have before, and that means I can like other people."

Huntercombe and Thorn Cross in Cheshire have also seen better-than-average results with reoffending—15- to 21-year-olds reoffend at a rate of 80 per cent nationally. Mink Lees talks of "changing hearts and minds through showing my trainees that we are with them rather than against them, because so many have had brutality, humiliation, contempt, and the feeling that they are useless and hopeless banged into them throughout their young lives".

I am convinced that humanity and real care, delivered by staff who have chosen to work with children and are trained to understand them, can work, and make youngsters like Charmion reconsider their criminal lifestyle. Prison is not ideal. It is mad that children have to be put inside to get the "bit of parenting" that Steve Butler, another trainer at Huntercombe, talks of. It is dreadful that, for some youngsters, these prisons are the only places where they will receive education on terms that work for them, and learn that people will treat them with decency if they respond that way.

But until we, as a society, become more interested in the youngsters who go wrong, more willing to use our voices, votes and taxes to improve the lot of the most marginalised and excluded children so that crime does not seem the only way to live their lives, prison remains the place where they will go.

Keeping the idea of prison as a place where the very best practice must be observed, where conditions are monitored constantly, where our young people are given opportunities to like themselves, where in fact it can do good to children, is all-important. There should be no taboo on discussing prison as a place for kids.

Gangs That Ravage Communities Need to Be Met with Fierce Penalties

Dianne Feinstein

Dianne Feinstein has been a U.S. senator from California since 1992.

On September 24 of this year [2006], Los Angeles experienced a new low. Three-year old Kaitlyn Avila was shot point-blank by a gang member who mistakenly thought her father was a member of a rival gang. The gang member shot and wounded her father, then intentionally fired into little Kaitlyn's chest. This is the first time law enforcement officials remember a young child being "targeted" in a gang shooting.

This shooting is but a symptom of the disease that has taken hold of our cities—and that disease is gang violence. The violence perpetrated by gang members on one another, on police officers and on innocent bystanders is horrifying.

Gang violence is an attack not only on individuals, but also on our communities. It stops mothers from allowing their children to play outside. It prevents the elderly from taking walks in their neighborhoods. It creates an environment of fear.

Gang Violence Is a National Problem

It is well past time for the federal government to provide a hand of assistance to state and local law enforcement. It is well past time to come to grips with the escalating levels of violence.

The key is a balanced, comprehensive approach.

Dianne Feinstein, keynote address at the Northern California Gang Prevention Summit, October 23, 2006. http://feinstein.senate.gov.

First, we must help those on the front lines. This means new laws, tougher penalties, and millions for investigations and prosecutions.

Second, we must identity and fund successful community programs. These are programs like the Gang Risk Intervention Program (GRIP) at Lennox Middle School in Inglewood [California], which I visited in August. The program's results are clear: 80 percent of participants graduated high school and stayed away from gangs. Students in the program were truant less often, and also showed improvement in their work habits and grades. We've got to replicate successful programs like this one across the country.

And third, we must make it safer for witnesses to come forward and testify. You can't win cases if witnesses fear for their life.

Many of you know that I've been working on gang legislation for several years. Yet, the bill has not become law.

So today, I'd like to talk about the scope of the problem; to let you know what I believe can be done to help stem the tide; and to ask for your help in getting a new, comprehensive law approved.

[Gangs] traffic in drugs, theft, extortion, prostitution, guns and murder.

The latest FBI [Federal Bureau of Investigation] statistics are in. Violent crime is on the rise—Murders are up. Robberies are up. Aggravated assaults are up. This is true in every region in the country, and the increases are greater than any year since 1991.

And a big reason for the rise? Gangs have metastasized from the big cities like Los Angeles and Chicago to the medium and small ones. Places like Milwaukee [Wisconsin], Birmingham [Alabama], Cleveland [Ohio], and St. Louis [Missouri].

There are now at least 30,000 gangs nationwide, with 800,000 members.

In California, there are 3,700 gangs up and down the State; 171,000 juveniles and adults are committed to this criminal way of life. That's greater than the population of 28 counties, and the same number of people that live in the City of Tracy.

You are all too aware of the damage that gangs do. From 1992 to 2003, there were more than 7,500 gang-related homicides reported in California. That's equivalent to the entire city of Sausalito.

And in 2004, more than one-third (of the 2,000) homicides in California (698) were gang-related. It's worse among our young. Nearly 50 percent of the murders of 18–29 year olds were gang-related. And nearly 60 percent of the murders of teens under 18 were gang-related.

Simply put, we would try to replicate and expand the state and local models that have worked in the past.

Now, the rate of gang violence is not always the same everywhere. There has been a recent drop in gang membership and gang violence in Los Angeles, for example. This is good news, but it is likely just a blip on the radar. Gang roots run deep in Los Angeles, and these gains may only be temporary.

Gang Members Routinely Murder Innocent People

When you look at the big picture, you see that gangs continue to infiltrate our communities. It is estimated that gangs are now having an impact on at least 2,500 communities across the nation. They control neighborhoods through violence. They traffic in drugs, theft, extortion, prostitution, guns, and murder.

All too often this puts law enforcement in danger. Let me name but a few:

- Los Angeles Police Officer Ricardo Lizarraga. Killed while responding to a domestic violence call, by a man who drew a gun and shot him twice in the back. The suspect was a known member of the Rollin20s Bloods.
- Merced Police Officer Stephan Gray. Officer Gray was shot and killed when a suspect (a gang member he had encountered before) fired two bullets into his chest.

The list goes on:

- Los Angeles Sherriff's Deputy Jeffrey Ortiz;
- Burbank Police Officer Matthew Pavelka;
- California Highway Patrol Officer Thomas Steiner; and
- San Francisco Police Officer Isaac Espinoza.

Los Angeles Police Department Chief Bill Bratton put it bluntly: "There is nothing more insidious than these gangs. They are worse than the Mafia. Show me a year in New York where the Mafia indiscriminately killed 300 people. You can't."

The problem is immense. It is on the streets. It is in the prisons. It is in big cities and small. It is in California, and every other state. So we've got to come up with a comprehensive approach.

Here are the key questions:

- How do we keep our youth out of these gangs in the first place?
- How do we encourage and protect witnesses who come forward and testify?
- And what do we do when the gangs perpetrate violence in our communities?

It is clear to me that a commitment has to be made on each of these fronts.

We know that a coordinated approach like this works. You have no further to look than Modesto for results:

In Modesto, community leaders put in place a model built on suppression, intervention and prevention. They established a law enforcement task force. They brought together police, sheriff, the DA [district attorney], parole, and corrections. They were able to create a database on gang members and use that shared intelligence to coordinate enforcement efforts. They established a community task force to make sure every elementary school had an after-school prevention program. They put sheriff's deputies into the middle and high schools, creating a constant visual presence.

This balanced approach has worked. Murders have dropped from 24 in 2003 and 2004 to only six in 2005 and 2006. Drive-by shootings have fallen 88 percent. Gang-related gun assaults have dropped by two-thirds from their peak.

Today's federal street gang laws are weak, and are almost never used.

The gang bill I am sponsoring would encourage this kind of balanced approach.

Federal Funds Are Critical to Reducing Violence

Senator Orrin Hatch of Utah and I first introduced legislation in 1996. And I have introduced a gang bill in each Congress since that time. Along the way, we have gotten close.

Many of the provisions of our gang bill were incorporated into the 1999 Juvenile Justice bill, which was approved overwhelmingly (73–25) by the Senate in the 106th Congress. But the bill stalled in Conference, and these provisions were never signed into law.

In 2004, our bill was approved by the Senate Judiciary Committee, but once again it stalled. And in this Congress, we worked with members of both sides of the aisle to develop a bill that enjoys broader support than we have had in the past. And we will reintroduce this legislation in the early days of the next Congress.

So what would this bill do?

Simply put, it would be a balanced program—with new programs and funding for prosecutions, and support for programs to prevent people from joining gangs in the first place.

The Department of Justice [DOJ] announced this Spring [2006] that it was devoting $30 million in new funds to fight gangs, including $2.5 million in Los Angeles. This is welcome, but it is but a drop in the bucket.

So the bill I have introduced would authorize almost 30 times the DOJ's initiative—$870 million for all activities over five years. $500 million of that would be used to create new "High Intensity Interstate Gang Activity Areas."

Bottom line: the growth in size and complexity of gangs has become a national problem, requiring a federal response.

These would mirror the successful HIDTA (High Intensity Drug Trafficking Area) model that brings together federal, state and local agents to coordinate investigations and prosecutions. And the $500 million would be split 50/50, so that for every dollar spent on law enforcement, a dollar would be spent on prevention.

Simply put, we would try to replicate and expand the state and local models that have worked in the past. And we would establish a clearinghouse to collect "best practices," so that this isn't theory, but what works on the street.

The bill would also authorize $100 million for Project Safe Neighborhoods, a Justice Department program designed to reduce gun violence in America.

Tougher Laws for Gang Members Are Needed

But at the same time, this bill would establish new crimes and tougher federal penalties.

Today's federal street gang laws are weak, and are almost never used. Currently, a person committing a gang crime might have extra time tacked on to the end of their federal sentence. This is because federal law currently focuses on gang violence as a sentencing enhancement, rather than a crime unto itself.

So the bill I have offered would make it a separate federal crime for any criminal street gang member to commit, conspire or attempt to commit violent crimes—including murder, kidnapping, arson, extortion—in furtherance of the gang.

And the penalties for gang members committing such crimes would increase considerably.

- For gang-related murder, the penalty would be life imprisonment or the death penalty.
- For kidnapping, aggravated sexual abuse or maiming, or if death resulted, the penalties would be from 5 years to life imprisonment.
- For any other serious violent felony, the penalty would be 3–30 years.
- And for any crime of violence—defined as the actual or intended use of physical force against the person of another—the penalty would run from 0–20 years.

The bill would also:

- Create a new crime for recruiting juveniles and adults into a criminal street gang. Currently, there is no federal crime that covers this.
- This bill would change that, by making recruiting gang members a new federal crime, with a penalty of 0–10

years. If someone recruited a minor, the penalty would be 1–20 years. And if someone recruited from prison, the penalty would be 5–20 years, and would be consecutive to their existing sentence.

- The bill would create new federal crimes for:
- committing multiple interstate murders;
- crossing state lines to obstruct justice; and
- committing violent crimes in connection with drug trafficking (whether or not it is gang-related).
- The bill would also increase the penalties for "RICO" (Racketeering Influenced and Corrupt Organizations)–related crimes, so that they match the new penalties the bill establishes for gang crimes.

States Cannot Solve Gang Problems on Their Own

This balanced approach—of prevention plus tough penalties—will send a clear message to gang members. Hardened gang members can take advantage of the opportunities we are creating, with schools and social services agencies empowered to make alternatives to gangs a realistic option. But if they continue to engage in violence, they will face serious consequences.

The bill would also provide $270 million in funds for witness protection grants. Too often, witnesses are afraid to come forward and tell the truth due to fear.

State and local law enforcement officers lack the resources needed to protect the safety of such witnesses and informants. So this legislation will be a clear-eyed approach to tackle all aspects of the problem.

Bottom line: the growth in size and complexity of gangs has become a national problem, requiring a federal response.

As long as I am a member of the United States Senate, I will make it one of my highest priorities to make that federal response a reality.

Violent Teen Criminals Need Adult Justice

Harry L. Shorstein

Harry L. Shorstein is the state attorney for the Fourth Judicial Circuit of Florida.

If the attempt to rehabilitate juvenile delinquents is unsuccessful, then it is my firm belief that we should treat habitual and violent juvenile criminals as adults. We aggressively direct-file habitual and violent juvenile offenders as adults and place them in jail or prison. This is the only way to effectively protect the public and is certainly more effective than leaving them in the juvenile justice system where they often bounce from rehabilitative program to program without any positive results. . . .

Adult Jail Time for Juveniles Is Effective

When I took office, our City [Jacksonville, Florida] was faced with a twenty-seven percent increase in the number of juveniles arrested from 1990 to 1991. Since then, we have prosecuted over 2,600 juvenile cases in adult court. Since 1993 alone, 1,178 juveniles prosecuted by my office have been incarcerated in the Duval County Jail and another 327 juveniles have been sentenced to extended time in the Florida State Prison, including twenty-four violent juveniles sentenced to life in prison. Our goal, of course, is to succeed in our prevention efforts and never be forced to prosecute a juvenile as an adult. Our statistics in this regard are very promising! In 1993, we referred 483 cases to adult court. In 2005, even with tougher laws mandating adult prosecution in certain cases, we only transferred 48 juvenile cases to adult court, the fewest transfers since I took office fifteen years ago!

Harry L. Shorstein, "Statement on Juvenile Justice," executive summary, State Attorney, Fourth Judicial Circuit of Florida, September, 2006, pp. 14–23. www.coj.net.

Our arrest statistics also prove that my philosophy has made a difference. After full implementation of our program, Jacksonville experienced an approximate thirty percent decrease in juvenile arrests from 1993 to 1994. This decrease included a forty-four percent reduction in the juvenile violent crime index (includes juveniles arrested for murder, aggravated assault, robbery, and sex crimes). During this same period, juvenile arrests went up statewide and nationwide. . . .

In recent years, the trend in Jacksonville has continued. From 1997 to 2005 overall juvenile arrests in Jacksonville were down twenty percent. . . .

To further increase the chances for success for juvenile inmates when they are released, we place a special emphasis on literacy.

My primary duty as State Attorney is to help protect the public. Incarceration of certain juveniles as adults is a necessary element of this function. However, the public is best served by efforts to turn around juvenile offenders before it is too late. . . .

Counseling and Programs in Jail

Simply warehousing juveniles in jail is not a long-term answer. With this in mind, the Director of our Juvenile Justice Divisions chairs a committee of professionals that constantly reevaluates programs in the jail designed to combine punishment and rehabilitation. . . .

In September 2003, the Cultural Council, through a grant from the National Endowment for the Arts and the State of Florida, began the "Living Inside" program in the jail. The program provides instruction to juvenile inmates in the areas of creative writing, photography and web design. The inspiring work of the juveniles who participated in the program can be viewed on their own website which can be accessed at www

.culturalcouncil.org. "Living Inside" continues to be funded through a private donation and a grant from the City of Jacksonville.

The cultural component of our program also includes theatrical productions. Theatreworks, a local theatrical group, has presented shows including a one man show about historical African-American sports heroes, "Goldrush," a show about losing freedom and new beginnings, and "Freedom Train," the story Harriet Tubman in the jail. . . .

The importance of these theatrical programs is not the entertainment value for the juveniles. The week before each performance, the teachers in the jail school use a curriculum that covers the history and social significance of the stories depicted. The shows are also an opportunity to exhibit a constructive manner of expression and to teach these young men how to behave properly in a social setting.

In addition to an education and assistance from social services, juvenile offenders need support and positive role models in order to better themselves.

Education in Jail

On August 3, 1993, I appeared before the Duval County School Board and urged them to provide education to the jailed juveniles. As a result, all juveniles in jail now attend school in jail as they would if they were in a regular school (assuming they were not truants). The juveniles receive full credit for what they successfully accomplished in school while incarcerated. To further increase the chances for success for juvenile inmates when they are released, we place a special emphasis on literacy. We have partnered with Learn to Read, whose volunteers tutor juveniles with particularly poor reading skills. Learn to Read has implemented a six-week program designed to meet the needs of juveniles with severe reading deficiencies.

In an effort to encourage reading, the school staff utilizes 1,500 books donated by our public libraries. A book club was created in the jail for inmates by a group of volunteers including a University of North Florida English professor, a music teacher, and a retired journalist. . . .

On June 9, 1995, we witnessed the fruits of our labors when five juvenile inmates who took advantage of their opportunities graduated from high school in a complete graduation ceremony held in the jail. Since 1995, we have continued to hold academic ceremonies in the jail. More than one hundred twenty-five juveniles have either graduated from high school, earned a GED [General Equivalency Diploma] certificate or received awards for academic achievement while incarcerated. At one jail graduation ceremony, the keynote speaker was a juvenile who had previously graduated from high school while incarcerated. On May 17, 2005, we reached another milestone in our program's history when twelve juvenile inmates were honored for earning a high school diploma or a GED. Betty Seabrook Burney, a local School Board member and a volunteer in the jail, gave a moving commencement address to the graduates. Mrs. Burney has been so moved by her involvement with the Juveniles in our program that she wrote the book *If These Chains Could Talk*. The book captures personal letters written by juvenile inmates concerning the poor choices they have made while offering real life insights that can prevent criminal behavior. A preview of the book can be seen on the web at www.talkingchains.com. This past May 2006, Mrs. Burney awarded and honored another eight juvenile inmates who earned either a GED or a high school diploma.

Mentors Work with Juvenile Offenders

In addition to an education and assistance from social services, juvenile offenders need support and positive role models in order to better themselves. It is with these needs in mind, that my staff organized the Jailed Juvenile Mentor Program. Volunteer mentors are recruited from throughout the community including the military, local organizations, the Chamber of Commerce and faith institutions. We have also formed a partnership with 100 Black Men of Jacksonville, who provide additional trained mentors to our program. This service agency makes scholarship money available to juvenile inmates qualified for college. The mentors visit the inmates a minimum of one hour per week at the jail. Positive bonds are made and our hope is the juveniles will learn there is another road they can take. These bonds continuc after the juveniles are released from jail. As an example, one mentor served as the best man in the wedding of a former inmate he has worked with for over three years. . . .

In 1997, we implemented a new group mentorship program known as Inside/Outside. Inside/Outside is a group of volunteers associated with local churches and synagogues who meet with juveniles in the jail once a week. The group continues to meet monthly with the juveniles after they complete their jail sentences. The "outside" portion of the program is designed to build on relationships developed during the sessions in the jail. The volunteers work to create a sense of community and to provide a "safe place" for juveniles who are facing the challenge of rejecting the negative influences that often await them in their home communities. An example of the positive influence of this group was when adult members of the group took two juveniles on probation to Alabama to help families whose homes were damaged by a tornado.

Once juveniles are released, they are supervised by specialized probation officers with reduced case loads.

In an effort to enhance the quality of the time our volunteers spend with the juveniles, we began the "Menders and Mentors" Program. As a part of this program, juveniles and their mentors work together on community service projects. As an example, recently, eight former jailed juveniles and their mentors assisted Builders Care (a nonprofit organization that provides emergency construction services to low-income, elderly and disabled people) with the final construction stages of a home for a disabled couple. I know that if we can make these troubled youth a part of the solution instead of the problem, we can help to turn them around. . . .

Juveniles Receive Special Support When They Are Released

Most juveniles are placed on probation after being released from jail. Before their release, a pre-release staffing is held for each juvenile. The purpose of the staffing is to let the probation officer, the juvenile's parents or guardians and the juvenile's mentor know what the child has accomplished in the jail programs and what will be expected of him while he is on probation. Multiple agencies are represented at the pre-release staffing, including the School Board, social service agencies providing counseling in the jail, the Department of Corrections and my office. A representative from the Boys and Girls Club also participates in the pre-release staffings. The Boys and Girls Club provides additional aftercare services to the juveniles by connecting them with their sites located throughout the city. . . .

Once juveniles are released, they are supervised by specialized probation officers with reduced case loads. As a part of probation, each juvenile is ordered to continue his education. Every effort is made to get the child back in school if this can be done without risk to other students. When appropriate, vocational education or other alternatives are explored. A caseworker from Communities in Schools (CIS), a national dropout prevention program also works with our program. CIS regularly brings speakers to the jail to address topics such as education and male responsibility. Each year, CIS organizes an end of the year celebration that honors the juvenile inmates for their academic achievements. After juveniles are released from the jail, CIS works to place them in an appropriate educational program and match them with needed community resources including job opportunities.

I am convinced that the proper combination of punishment, constructive programming and after care will turn criminals into productive citizens.

There are several other special conditions of each child's probation, including getting a part-time job and abiding by a curfew. If a juvenile needs psychological help or special services such as anger control classes or substance abuse treatment, he is ordered to participate. Because of the uniqueness of our program, the Department of Corrections funds advanced counseling services for juveniles on probation. The "Case Management Program" provides comprehensive evaluation and counseling for juvenile offenders free of charge.

The Department of Corrections reports that many juveniles who have left the jail have turned their lives around. These former criminals have graduated from high school, obtained jobs and are productive members of society. The most significant and pleasing proof that our program is working is the reduction in the number of juveniles meeting our criteria for prosecution as an adult and the resulting tremendous decrease in the population of juveniles at the jail. Nationwide, the number of juveniles in jail increased nearly ninety percent between 1993 and 1998. Although the number of juveniles in jail has dropped since peaking in the late 1990's, there was still a sixty-five percent increase nationwide between 1993 and 2004. In our program, despite expansion in the criteria qualifying a juvenile for prosecution as an adult, the number of juveniles in our jail has decreased from a high of 200 in 1994 to a current average of less than fifty! Since my philosophy remains the same, the only explanation is a decrease in the number of juveniles committing offenses which would qualify them for prosecution in adult court. It is critical to understand that the purpose of our juvenile justice program is to reduce crime. *Not* to increase the number of children incarcerated. I am convinced that the proper combination of punishment, constructive programming and after care will turn criminals into productive citizens. . . .

What Others Are Saying

Periodically, members of my staff speak with juveniles in the jail in an effort to learn what we can do to turn at-risk youths around before they need to be incarcerated. These juvenile inmates tell us that they need positive role models, recreation opportunities and after-school programs. They also tell us that they learned at an early age that there were no consequences for their criminal behavior. I believe that through our community involvement, our intervention programs and through aggressive prosecution we are responding to these challenges and are making a difference.

The problem of juvenile crime has not been solved. However, the combination of early intervention for at-risk youth and swift, hard punishment for juvenile criminals is working in our community. We have shown that if we let common sense and not rhetoric guide the system we can greatly reduce juvenile crime. I believe our system can serve as a model for the rest of the State and the Nation. Our office has received international attention and acclaim for our programs. I welcome this opportunity to show others there are logical answers.

Organizations to Contact

The editors have compiled the following list of organizations concerned with the issues debated in this book. The descriptions are derived from materials provided by the organizations. All have publications or information available for interested readers. The list was compiled on the date of publication of the present volume; the information provided here may change. Be aware that many organizations take several weeks or longer to respond to inquiries, so allow as much time as possible.

The Brady Center to Prevent Gun Violence
1225 Eye St. NW, Suite 1100, Washington, DC 20005
(202) 289-7319 • fax: (202) 408-1851
Web site: www.bradycenter.org/index.php

The Brady Center is devoted to creating an America free from gun violence, where all Americans are safe at home, at school, at work, and in our communities. It works to enact and enforce sensible gun laws, regulations, and public policies through grassroots activism, electing public officials who support gun laws, and increasing public awareness of gun violence. The Brady Center has various brochures and publications that help educate the public.

Center for the Prevention of School Violence (CPSV)
1801 Mail Service Center, Raleigh, NC 27699-1801
(800) 299-6054
e-mail: megan.q.howell@ncmail.net
Web site: www.ncdjjdp.org/cpsv

The center's efforts are directed at understanding the problems of school violence and developing solutions to them. Positive youth development efforts are emphasized as the center focuses beyond the school into the community and works in support of youth-serving programs and agencies that target the development of attitudes, behaviors, and conditions that enable youth to grow and become productive members of their communities. Numerous publications and resources are available.

Center for the Study and Prevention of Violence (CSPV)
University of Colorado at Boulder, 1877 Broadway, Suite 601
Boulder, CO 80302
(303) 492-1032 • fax: (303) 443-3297
e-mail: cspv@colorado.edu
Web site: www.colorado.edu/cspv

CSPV's goal is to provide informed assistance to groups committed to understanding and preventing violence, particularly adolescent violence. In an effort to establish more complete and valuable information to impact violence-related policies, programs, and practices, CSPV works from a multidisciplinary platform on the subject of violence and facilitates the building of bridges between the research community and the practitioners and policy makers. It collects research literature and resources on the causes and prevention of violence and provides direct information services to the public by offering topical searches on customized databases.

Center on Juvenile and Criminal Justice (CJCJ)
54 Dore St., San Francisco, CA 94103
(415) 621-5661 • fax: (415) 621-5466
email: dmacallair@cjcj.org
Web site: www.cjcj.org

CJCJ seeks to reduce society's reliance on the use of incarceration as a solution to social problems. CJCJ offers various reports, fact sheets, and articles relating to juvenile justice.

Children Now
1212 Broadway, 15th Floor, Oakland, CA 94612
(510) 763-2444 • fax: (510) 763-1974
e-mail: info@childrennow.org
Web site: www.childrennow.org

This is a research and action organization dedicated to assuring that children grow up in economically secure families, where parents can go to work confident that their children are supported by quality health coverage, a positive media environment, a good early education, and safe, enriching activities after school. Strategies are designed to improve children's lives while at the same time help America build a sustained commitment to putting children first. The organization publishes a biennial California County Data Book that contains county-level statistics about California children.

Juvenile Justice Initiative (JJI)
413 West Monroe, Springfield, IL 62704
(217) 522-7970 • fax: (217) 522-7980
e-mail: mreynoldsjuv@yahoo.com or bcjuv@aol.com
Web site: www.jjustice.org

JJI is a statewide advocacy coalition to transform the juvenile justice system. The JJI advocates to reduce reliance on detention, to enhance fairness for all youth, and to develop adequate community-based resources throughout Illinois. JJI publishes newsletters and reports throughout the year.

Mothers Against Violence in America (MAVIA)
105 14th Ave., Suite 2A, Seattle, WA 98122
(206) 323-2303 • fax: (206) 323-2132
e-mail: info@mavia.org
Web site: www.mavia.org

MAVIA prevents violence by and against children through education, outreach and advocacy, and encourages individuals to take personal responsibility for creating safe communities and schools. Various publications are available.

National Alliance for Safe Schools (NASS)
PO Box 290, Slanesville, WV 25444-0290
(304) 496-8100 • fax: (304) 496-8105
e-mail: NASS@raven-villages.net
Web site: www.safeschools.org

NASS is a research and information arm of the National Association of School Safety and Law Enforcement Officers. It works to help school administrators and staff improve their methods for maintaining safe and secure learning environments; designs, tests, and implements crime prevention and disciplinary models for public school systems; provides assistance with security assessments of school districts, and conducts research into strategies for combating particular problems. Publications include *Making Schools SAFE for Students* and *Emergency Management Plan.*

National Alliance of Gang Investigators' Associations (NAGIA)
PO Box 608628, Orlando, FL 32860-8628
(321) 388-8694 • fax (407) 836-3103
e-mail: RustyKeeble@fgia.com
Web site: www.nagia.org

NAGIA promotes and coordinates national antigang strategies, advocating for standardization of antigang training, establishment of uniform gang definitions, assistance for communities with emerging gang problems, and input to policy makers and program administrators. NAGIA participated in the *National Gang Threat Assessment* (April 2005) report and maintains an online library of articles written by gang specialists from around the United States on a variety of gang-related topics.

National Association of School Resource Officers (NASRO)
1951 Woodlane Dr., St. Paul, MN 55125
888-316-2776 • fax: (651) 457-5665
email: kevin.quin@nasro.org
Web site: www.nasro.org

NASRO consists of school resource/police officers, school administrators, juvenile detectives, school security officers, and DARE (Drug Abuse Resistance Education) officers. NASRO seeks to build a rapport between law enforcement officers and America's youth, while providing safe and secure learning environments. The organization publishes *Resourcer*, a quarterly newsletter.

National School Safety Center
141 Duesenberg Dr., Suite 11, Westlake Village, CA 91362
(805) 373-9977 • fax: (805) 373-9277
Web site: www.schoolsafety.us/home.php

The National School by working to prevent Safety Center serves as an advocate for safe, secure, and peaceful schools worldwide school crime and violence. The center identifies and promotes strategies, practices, and programs that support safe schools for all students as part of the total academic mission. Publications, videos, and training assistance are available. Their work products, training, technical assistance, and consultation services are designed to support safe school planning activities.

National Youth Violence Prevention Resource Center (NYVPRC)
PO Box 10809, Rockville, MD 20849-0809
(866) 723-3968 • fax: (301) 562-1001
Web site: www.safeyouth.org/scripts/index.asp

NYVPRC offers information on youth violence and referrals to organizations providing youth violence prevention and intervention services. It is a gateway for professionals, parents, youth, and other interested individuals, and offers the latest tools to facilitate discussion with children, to resolve conflicts nonviolently, to stop bullying, to prevent teen suicide, and to end violence committed by and against young people. Resources include fact sheets, best practices documents, funding and conference announcements, statistics, research bulletins, surveillance reports, and profiles of promising programs.

Peace Games
280 Summer St., Mezzanine Level, Boston, MA 02210
(617) 261-3833 • fax: (617) 261-6444
e-mail: info@peacegames.org
Web site: www.peacegames.org

Peace Games provides a number of resources to communities and schools to help them foster communication, cooperation, conflict resolution, and civic engagement in students and adults alike. It offers a spectrum of services from one-time training to a full three-year Peace Games partnership. Peace Games provides expertise and experience in creating and sustaining a culture of peace in a school setting. Various articles are available.

Prevention Institute
265 29th St., Oakland, CA 94611
(510) 444-7738 • fax: (510) 663-1280
Web site: www.preventioninstitute.org

The Prevention Institute has worked on violence prevention projects in numerous capacities, including facilitating violence prevention collaboratives, conducting research and writing, evaluating violence prevention efforts, and conducting strategy development and training. It serves as a focal point for training in violence prevention through local, state, and national efforts. It works to prevent various forms of violence, such as youth violence, child abuse, rape and sexual assault, hate violence, and intimate-partner violence.

Stop the Violence, Face The Music (STV)
732 Casino Center Blvd., 2nd Fl.
Las Vegas, NV 89101-6716
(800)-732-6366 • fax: (877) 707-3417
e-mail: admin@stv.net
Web site: www.stv.net

STV counteracts the negative influences affecting youth by providing counseling and promoting messages for antiviolence, crime, and substance abuse through the use of educational programs, music, public service ads, and television campaigns. STV also publishes *Teenagers Guide to Surviving the Teenage Years*, which contains a collection of real-life stories that cover issues such as peer pressure, violence, prostitution, and sex.

Street Law
1010 Wayne Ave., Suite 870, Silver Spring, MD 20910
(301) 589-1130 • fax: (301) 589-1131
e-mail: clearinghouse@streetlaw.org
Web site: www.streetlaw.org

Street Law operates programs in law-related education (LRE) in high schools, juvenile corrections settings, and communities in the United States and around the world; it assists young people in becoming active, successful citizens through the study of LRE, where students learn substantive information about law, the legal system, and their rights and responsibilities through strategies that promote cooperative learning, critical thinking, and positive interaction between young people and adults. Street Law publishes *Street Law News*, a semiannual newsletter, and various articles and brochures.

Student Pledge Against Gun Violence (SPAGV)
112 Nevada St., Northfield, MN 55057
(507) 645-5378 • fax: (507) 663-1207
e-mail: mlgrow@pledge.org
Web site: www.pledge.org

SPAGV works to end gun violence among young people. It provides information and conducts events, programs, and activities for youth. It believes that young people, through their own decisions, can play a role in reducing gun violence. It refers teachers, counselors, and community leaders to valuable resources, includes curriculum suggestions that can be integrated with existing academic programs, and contains information about how schools can participate.

Violence Policy Center (VPC)
1730 Rhode Island Ave. NW, Suite 1014
Washington, DC 20036
(202) 822-8200 • fax: (202) 822-8205
e-mail: info@vpc.org
Web site: www.vpc.org

The VPC works to stop gun-related death and injury through research, advocacy, and education. It also works with national, state, and local advocacy organizations representing affected constituencies—such as women, children, minorities, consumers, and public health practitioners—to keep neighborhoods, homes, schools, and workplaces safe from gun violence. Each year, the VPC releases fact-based studies on a full range of gun violence issues.

Voices for America's Children (VAC)
1000 Vermont Ave. NW, 7th Floor, Washington, DC 20005
(202) 289-0777 • fax: (202) 289-0776
e-mail: voices@voices.org
Web site: www.childadvocacy.org

VAC serves as a forum for the exchange of ideas and information whose activities impact state and local public policy issues including basic income, family support service, child welfare, juvenile justice, education, health and nutrition, and child care. Its goals include increasing the ability of child advocacy organizations to influence public policy. It provides technical assistance to organizations involved in child advocacy, facilitates the exchange of assistance among members, and develops methods of increasing the availability and use of information on children's issues. VAC publishes an annual report.

Bibliography

Books

Craig A. Anderson et al.	*Violent Video Game Effects on Children and Adolescents: Theory, Research, and Public Policy*. New York: Oxford University Press, 2007.
Rami Benbenishty and Ron Avi Astor	*School Violence in Context: Culture, Neighborhood, Family, School, and Gender*. New York: Oxford University Press, 2005.
Ken Blanchard	*How to Talk to Your Kids About School Violence*. New York: Onomatopoeia, 2003.
Dewey G. Cornell	*School Violence: Fears Versus Facts*. Mahwah, NJ: Lawrence Erlbaum, 2006.
R. Barri Flowers	*Kids Who Commit Adult Crimes: Serious Criminality by Juvenile Offenders*. New York: Haworth, 2002.
Edwin R. Gerler	*Handbook of School Violence*. Binghamton, NY: Haworth Press, 2004.
Clive Harber	*Schooling as Violence: How Schools Harm Pupils and Societies*. New York: RoutledgeFalmer, 2004.
Mary Jo McGrath	*School Bullying: Tools for Avoiding Harm and Liability*. Thousand Oaks, CA: Corwin, 2006.

Mark Harrison Moore, et al., eds. *Deadly Lessons: Understanding Lethal School Violence*. New York: Joseph Henry Press, 2002.

Katherine S. Newman et al. *Rampage: The Social Roots of School Shootings*. New York: Basic Books, 2005.

Kathryn Seifert *How Children Become Violent: Keeping Your Kids Out of Gangs, Terrorist Organizations, and Cults*. New York: Acanthus, 2006.

Kathy Sexton-Radek *Violence in Schools: Issues, Consequences, and Expressions*. Westport, CT: Praeger, 2004.

R. Murray Thomas *Violence in America's Schools: Understanding, Prevention, and Responses*. Westport, CT: Praeger, 2006.

David Trend *The Myth of Media Violence: A Critical Introduction*. Oxford, UK: Blackwell, 2006.

Julie A. Webber *Failure to Hold: The Politics of School Violence*. Lanham, MD: Rowman & Littlefield, 2003.

Periodicals

Jackie M. Allen "Linking Spirituality and Violence Prevention in School Counseling," *Professional School Counseling*, June 1, 2004.

Earnestine Bennett-Johnson	"The Root of School Violence: Causes and Recommendations For a Plan of Action," *College Student Journal*, June 1, 2004.
Judy Brunner	"How to Assess and Respond to Student Threats," *Principal Leadership*, October 1, 2006.
William Jelani Cobb	"My So-Called Life: After Doing Time in an Adult Prison, Can This Teen Turn His Life Around?" *Essence*, June 1, 2004.
David Codrea	"Look Who's Demanding Gun Control," *Guns Magazine*, August 1, 2005.
Kim Gandy	"School Shooters Target Girls, Point to Larger Problem of Violence Against Women," *National NOW Times*, Winter 2007.
Susan Gilmore	"Converting Bullies with Books," *Christian Science Monitor*, April 9, 2003.
Thomas M. Gwaltney	"Violence Goes to School: Lessons Learned from Columbine," *Childhood Education*, July 1, 2004.
Scott W. Henggeler	"Conduct Disorder and Delinquency," *Journal of Marital and Family Therapy*, October 1, 2003.
Jeff Holtz	"Parents File Lawsuit Over Bullying of Daughter," *New York Times*, January 9, 2005.

Adrienne Jones — "Thwarting Bullies Proves Tough Work," *Age*, November 22, 2004.

Arthur Jones — "Ministry of Presence: Young People in Detention Need Someone to Care," *National Catholic Reporter*, May 28, 2004.

Jaana Juvonen et al. — "Bullying Among Young Adolescents: The Strong, the Weak, and the Troubled," *Pediatrics*, December 2003.

Patricia J. Kelly — "Health Promotion in the Juvenile Justice System," *Journal of Multicultural Nursing & Health*, Summer 2004.

Cathy Lanier — "Gun Control Laws Help Stop Youth Homicides," *Deseret News*, March 18, 2007.

Margaret Littman — "Sugar, Spice and Not Very Nice," *Chicago Tribune*, May 8, 2002.

Wade C. Mackey and Ronald S. Immerman — "The Presence of the Social Father in Inhibiting Young Men's Violence," *Mankind Quarterly*, Spring/Summer 2004.

Joyce Lee Malcolm — "Gun Control's Twisted Outcome: Restricting Firearms Has Helped Make England More Crime-Ridden Than the U.S.," *Reason*, November 1, 2002.

Susannah Meadows — "Ghosts of Columbine," *Newsweek*, November 3, 2003.

Matt Olson	"Kids in the Hole—Juvenile Offenders," *Progressive*, August 2003.
Carole Rayburn	"Assessing Students for Morality Education: A New Role for School Counselors," *Professional School Counseling*, June 2004.
Michael H. Romanowski	"Is School Prayer the Answer?" *Educational Forum*, Winter 2002.
J. Brad Shepherd et al.	"Level of Functioning and Recidivism Risk Among Adolescent Offenders," *Adolescence*, Spring 2005.
Amy L. Sherman	"Mentoring on the Margins: A Ministry to Public Schools," *Christian Century*, January 11, 2005.
Greg Toppo	"Troubling Days at U.S. Schools," *USA Today*, October 21, 2003.
Claudia Wallis and Kristina Dell	"What Makes Teens Tick," *Time*, May 10, 2004.
Marti Yarbrough	"Movies, Music & TV: Can Parents Monitor Their Children's Entertainment?" *Jet*, March 28, 2005.

Index

C

D

E

F

G

S

W

Y

Z